The Prayer of the Heart

The Foundational Spiritual Mystery at the Core of Christianity

By Alphonse and Rachel Goettmann

Translated by
Theodore and Rebecca Nottingham

ISBN 9780615986654

Translated from the original French, *Prière de Jésus: Prière de Coeur.*

Éditions Dervy, 1988; Albin Michel, 1995.

TABLE OF CONTENTS

Translator's Note 5

Introduction by George A. Maloney, S.J. 7

Preface..15

Chapter One: The Power of the Name in the Old and

New Testaments 17

Chapter Two: The Jesus Prayer in

the Early Tradition 35

 1 The Birth of the Prayer of the Heart

 2 Mount Sinai

3 St. Symeon the New Theologian

4 Mount Athos

5 The Philokalia and The Way of the Pilgrim

6 Modern Times

Chapter Three: The Practice of the Jesus Prayer 59

Chapter Four: The Jesus Prayer as a Way of Life 99

Chapter Five: The Path of Conversion

and Asceticism 147

1 Gluttony

2 Lewdness

3 Avarice

4 Sadness

5 Anger

6 Sloth

7 Vanity

8 Pride

9 Watchfulness

Chapter Six: The Meaning of the Prayer 191

1 "Lord"

2 "Jesus"

3 "Jesus Christ"

4 "Son of God

5 "Have Mercy on Me, a Sinner"

TRANSLATOR'S NOTE

by Theodore J. Nottingham

This book changed my life. It introduced me to the ancient spiritual tradition of the Christian faith which has been virtually lost to the West for the last thousand years. In this work, we find both a history and a practical guide for the application of the Prayer to one's daily life.

The teaching contained in these pages has been handed down through the centuries like a torch passed on in the night. We owe its survival to souls marked by astonishing devotion and illumination who have lived the Prayer so intensely that their influence is still a great beacon for our times.

The Prayer of the Heart is key to the state of ceaseless prayer that awakens people to continual remembrance of God. This is consciousness of the divine in every moment is the response to the admonition to "seek first the Kingdom." Life is then truly given in abundance through Grace that blesses those who open their hearts and minds to the reality of God. Such a way of life can lead Christians into an authentic encounter with the living Christ.

INTRODUCTION

by George A. Maloney, S.J.

God is again calling His people into the desert. And there He wishes to reveal Himself in a powerful, unifying way beyond words and images, in the immediacy of a lover to His beloved.

Like Moses in the desert, tending Jethro's flocks, these people are hearing God's command to strip themselves of every control they have over their lives. Moses heard God's command to take off his shoes. When he did, a new revelation of God came over him. God revealed Himself to Moses as a burning, devouring fire.

His first impulse was one of curiosity. He wanted to go forward by his own powers in order to comprehend the exterior "why" of God through his reasoning powers. But he learned that the first step necessary to receive God's intimate revelation of Himself was to be stripped, unencumbered by his own self. Moses became God's prophet when he was completely purified in his heart, having taken off his shoes, leaving behind all of his securities and protections.

God is not a land to be conquered by our human force. He is a holy land, which we moderns approach with bare feet, a symbol of the total ineffectiveness of our own power, a sign of purity of heart.

Searching for a Deeper Form of Christianity.

Today many Christians are tired of living double lives, part-time as Christ-centered humans and part-time as world-centered citizens. They desire to move beyond a surface Christianity and invite Jesus to become Lord and Master, even over their unconscious. They take seriously St. Paul's advice: "Be not conformed to this world, but be transformed by the renewal of your mind" (Rom. 12:2). They are tired of living their Christianity in such a superficial way that when the thin veneer is scratched, a whole area of interior darkness, selfishness, prejudice and resentment is exposed as unhealed.

 The best way to clean the surface of a lake is not by skimming the top but by purifying the source of the flow from the wellsprings at the bottom. In all of us there are hidden recesses in our unconscious which the healing power of Jesus Christ has not yet touched.

A Growth in Greater Personalism

We see taking place, throughout the whole Church and throughout all society, what Teilhard de Chardin called the process of convergence and of "hominization"; the process whereby the human race is consciously growing into a global village. We human beings are our brothers and 'sisters' keepers, wherever in this whole universe they may be found.

Hence, in the thrust toward a new and greater awareness of the value of each human person, we see that we must move toward a greater in-depth, personal prayer. We can see that the basis for this more contemplative type of prayer is the integration of body, soul and spirit. Today western Christians are using Yoga, Zen and other transcendental techniques, especially the breathing techniques, the emptying of the mind through a process of relaxation, as standard equipment for the contemplative life. This thrust toward greater personalism in one's prayer can also explain the recent discovery of the Jesus Prayer — or the Prayer of the Heart — by those Christians who seriously seek a more personal contact with the Lord.

The Philokalia, an eighteenth-century collection of writings of the early Desert Fathers who practiced the Jesus Prayer, has preserved for us the tradition of those early Christian athletes who, intoxicated by God's love for them, repeated day and night the prayer: "Lord Jesus Christ, Son of God, have mercy on me, a sinner." To these simple "children of the kingdom of heaven," the Spirit revealed the essence of the Jesus-event in a living experience.

They were, indeed, "Jesus people," whose love for Him was more durable than a mere fad. These were the charismatics of the early period of Christianity who, when baptized in the Holy Spirit, experienced, as we still can do today, a vivid realization of the power inherent in the name of Jesus. It is the spirit of the risen Jesus who reveals to us all we need to know of Jesus as our Lord and Savior (Jn. 14:26).

The Power of the Name of Jesus

These athletes of Christ knew from experience in the desert of their hearts that there is no other name whereby we are to be saved. Peter, after curing the cripple before the Beautiful Gate in Jerusalem, professed loudly: "It is the name of this same Jesus; it is faith in that name, which has cured this man" (Acts 3:16). We must do the same to the whole world.

They witnessed with Paul to the sacred power of that name. "God has given Him a name that is above all names so that at the name of Jesus every knee shall bend in heaven, on earth and under the earth" (Phil. 2:9–10).

The Prayer of the Heart

Hesychasm is an eastern Christian form of living the spiritual life that has its roots in the first hermits who fled into the barren deserts of Egypt and Syria during the fourth century and succeeding ages. It is a spiritual system of essentially contemplative orientation which finds the perfection of the human person in union with the Trinity through continuous prayer. Hesychasm comes from the Greek word *hesychia*. It means tranquility or peace. Hesychia is that state in which the Christian, through grace and his/her own intense asceticism, reintegrates his/her whole being into a single person who is placed completely under the direct influence of the Trinity dwelling within that person.

It stresses an entire way of life in Christ that strives for total, loving surrender to the indwelling Trinity through a vigorous, even militant discipline of body, soul and spirit that was summarized in gospel terms as "purity of heart." The heart, in scriptural language, is the seat of human life, of all that touches us in the depths of our personality — all affections, passions, desires, knowledge and thoughts. It is in our "heart" that we in prayer meet God in an I-Thou relationship. The heart, and not the mind, is considered in this spirituality of the Christian east, as the center of our being, that which directs us in our ultimate values and choices. It is the inner chamber where, in secret, the heavenly Father sees us through and through. It is where we attain inner honesty, humility, integration and purity of heart.

A New Articulation of Heart Spirituality

This heart spirituality, which is at the core of the Jesus Prayer, has been articulated by eastern Christian writers of the past in a language that grew out of desert monasticism. Its terminology, concepts and, above all, its applications have usually been a grave obstacle for modern Christians in finding much of what might be relevant for their spiritual lives. Modern Christians need an interpretation of heart spirituality that will speak to them in meaningful and practical ways.

Father Alphonse Goettmann, a French Orthodox priest, aided by his wife Rachel, offers in this volume just such a work. He is not only well-versed in the history of the spirituality of the Prayer of the Heart and its authors of the past but, as is evident in his writing, has personally immersed himself in living this spirituality. He and his wife share their life of heart-prayer with Christian pilgrims from all parts of the world who come to visit and live this ancient Christian spirituality in retreat at Bethanie, their Orthodox community near Metz in eastern France.

This volume, *The Prayer of the Heart*, is the result of their years of living and teaching others this ancient form of eastern Christian prayer out of the abundance of their deep spirituality. The co-authors offer chapters that deal with the power of the name of Jesus as found in the Old and New Testaments, a brief history of how the Jesus Prayer developed among the Eastern Fathers, then very practical, experiential chapters on the practice of the Prayer as a way of life. The reader is challenged to follow a continuous path of conversion and asceticism. A concluding chapter offers a meditative commentary on the traditional formula of the Jesus Prayer and its profound implications.

Any reader who brings a hunger to call upon the name and experience the presence of the risen Lord Jesus Christ will be abundantly rewarded. This book is more than another historical review of how monks of old, living in the desert, developed their lives from the gospels and prayed out the Jesus Prayer. It is more than a series of psychosomatic exercises, a how-to book teaching how to contact the indwelling Trinity by calling on Jesus as the way.

It is the wisdom of two persons who live the prayer of the heart spirituality in the twentieth century and humbly, but with fi ery poetry in their hearts, share the treasures of the ancient Christian east in a way that will speak powerfully and practically to moderns of both east and west. To the reader of this work, my hope and prayer is that your breath and heartbeat will become one with the name and presence of Jesus Christ so that you will be able to live consciously in His love and become His love to all you meet and serve. May this book teach you how to learn from the indwelling Trinity to pray incessantly (1 Th ess. 5:17).

PREFACE

By Father Alphonse and Rachel Goettmann

Bethanie in Gorze, France

We have dared to write a book on the Jesus Prayer because we are certain that it will become one of the most important keys to the rediscovery of the first spark of early Christianity. This effort is not a restitution of the past, but an entrance into the continuing creation of a Presence which has never left us.

The Jesus Prayer penetrates everything, freeing us from all the acculturations of the Gospel, re-creating the basis of unity for all Christians and offering them the only possible anchor for a true ecumenism.

The Jesus Prayer heals the alienation and distress of humanity, placing its dependence on God alone, substituting the divine life for the little "self" and the interests it must defend. "It is no longer I who live, but Christ who lives in me" (Gal 2:20). Here the incarnation continues and completes itself.

This book has grown out of lived experience and not out of theory. The Jesus Prayer has been the foundation of our lives for over forty years. But we have not taken a solitary path. This work is the fruit of twenty years of sharing with hundreds of people through retreats and sessions at Bethanie, a "place of rebirth" which we founded on the foundation of the Prayer. A community has been established there which seeks the dynamism of the first communities witnessed to in the Acts of the Apostles who "lived in the Name of Jesus."

The Jesus Prayer is a way of life, making us true disciples of Christ. It is a beacon for the people of God, leading them toward the promised land.

Chapter One

THE POWER OF THE NAME IN THE OLD
AND NEW TESTAMENTS

All who call upon the name of the Lord shall be delivered.

Joel 2:32

No one has ever seen God and no one knows His name — God is unnameable and indescribable. But our Creator has fashioned a place of intimate encounter within us so that we can always meet God and hear His voice. This sacred ground is the human heart, and everytime that we descend into it to honor God in His home, this encounter is called prayer. The Prayer of the Heart has existed, therefore, from the dawn of humanity. There is no true existence until we have discovered this place where we are forever born into the divine life. God calls us to life within our hearts and only those w who listen become fully human. This is our vocation.

That is why God's call to us resonates from one end of the Bible to the other: "Shema Israel!" That call contains the whole of our spiritual life. "Shema" means "Listen!" from the root shem which translates as "the name." To listen to the name of God in the depths of our heart is to be born anew, to receive the divine seed in which we discover our own true name, the person hidden deep within. Adam and Eve, the first humans, lived in such intimacy with God, receiving from Him "mouth-to-mouth," in a transfusion of breath as the Hebraic text says. But they very quickly refused to listen and the rupture was not long in coming. From that break came, in the second generation, the crime of Cain.

Instead of looking for the name of God within ourselves, we have ever since wanted another name and have, therefore, lost our inner axis. Uncentered, Cain scatters himself, building cultures and civilizations without God. This is the condition of humanity "chased out of Eden"; that is to say, chased out of ourselves and thereby losing our identity. God's response to such defiance was to maintain the covenant through giving a third son to Adam and Eve: Seth. A new line is then opened with the birth of Enoch, who the Bible calls "the first to invoke the name" after the fall (Gen. 4:26).

The path of return is, indeed, possible, and we become truly human through this invocation which is our ultimate fulfillment. "Enoch" means "Man"! In fact, the Semitic race begins with Shem, the first son of Noah — shem, the bearers of the name — and with that race is also born the distant tradition of the Jesus Prayer, whose disciples in turn "carry the name inscribed on their foreheads" (2 Rev. 14:1). This line of bearers of the name, from Genesis to Revelation, is never interrupted and so Christians are called to be the new Semites.

For the ancient Hebrews, the shem, the name, encompasses the secret nature of every being; it is its emanation, its active and mysterious presence. Active because it is through its name that a being manifests itself; mysterious because the name reveals the person. To know someone by his or her name is to know them to the core, in the place where he or she is unique. In the thought of the primitive Semite, he who reveals his name gives access to his most hidden transcendence. But by giving himself to others, he also becomes vulnerable. All the ancient religions knew this secret and knew that by invoking the name of their gods, they had an instrument of knowing and a new amazing power; that is why invocation was at the center of worship and of the fundamental religious attitude, often to the point of magic.

When Jacob (Gen. 32:20), Manoah (Judg. 13:17) and Moses (Ex. 3:9–15) ask God what His name is, it is precisely for the purpose of entering into the divine intimacy through the secret unveiled by the name, making it possible to follow Him. The people would only follow Moses through the dangers of the desert to the promised land because he was the bearer of that name who invested him with his mission. Indeed, "all the peoples go forward, each in the name of its god" (Mic. 4:5).

The revelation of the sacred name to Moses on Mount Horeb has a double characteristic. First, the "I Am" is received by Moses, heard by him at the heart of an experience of fire: the burning bush. God offers Himself to us in a name and in the very act of naming Himself. To perceive the name is a theophanic experience (a theophany is a manifestation or apparition of God), arousing fear and trembling before the sacred, that abyss opened by utter transcendence.

But Yahweh also reveals Himself in that same name as "I shall be with you" (Ex. 3:12). He is the wholly other, the beyond of all things, the inaccessible independence and sovereign liberty, Being itself. He is also the incandescent core of all that is, the Creator at the heart of the creature. He is present in all the strands of history of which He is the acting mystery, He who unveils His name as we explore the depths through a continual dialogue with Him in daily life.

 This faith in the power of the name, seen in all the biblical generations, is foundational in sacred history, in the personal history of our salvation as well as in general human history. Always present, consciously or not, it is the backdrop to all events and activities of the Hebrew people; of all that is said officially through the mouths of kings or in the secret whispers of nomads under their tents, of all that is not said and, in the depths of silence, this same faith is its ultimate meaning. The certainty of this faith is an experience for it depends not only on the promise of the Lord but especially on its realization through Isaac (Gen. 26:3–5) and Jacob (Gen. 28:15, 31:3–5), Moses (Ex. 3:12, 4:12), Gideon (Judg. 6:16), David (2 Sam. 7:9), and all the way down through the exiled (Is. 43:5).

These great events mark out the past of Israel and fertilize its present. The pious Jew in whose spirit is sown this "consciousness" knows how to read from moment to moment the revelation of the sacred name under the most ordinary appearances. He blesses everything, for everything is the burning bush. His life tends to become praise, and his mysticism blossoms in the "even though" and "in spite of" on the basis of this conviction. Even if everything points to the contrary, in the very center of the worst storms, when no event makes sense, even then he knows the "I am with you," and his response can only be: "In spite of it all, I love you." Wandering through trials that sometimes lead to martyrdom, such a person holds fast "as though he could see the invisible" (Heb. 11:23–26).

In this continual reciprocity is established the covenant within the heart where the progressive revelation of the name is witnessed. What is at stake in the epiphany of the name is this covenant forever offered by God to humanity. God courts us, searching us out and drawing us to Himself. He spells out His name to us, places it on the tongue and in the heart of Moses, hoping that all the people will invoke it and repeat it daily, like a fiancé looking forward to the wedding: "Yahweh, Yahweh, God of tenderness …" (Ex. 34:6). And God answers: "I will let all My splendor pass in front of you and I will pronounce before you the name of Yahweh … Here is a place beside Me" (Ex. 33:18–23).

All lovers recognize themselves in this relationship. "Give me a heart which loves," said Saint Augustine, "and that person will understand." We should not be surprised that, in such a relationship, God shows Himself so "jealous" toward all the false gods before which humanity prostrates itself! (Ex. 34:10–16). This is the jealousy of love which watches over its people. Yahweh will throw them into trials at every betrayal until they return at the remembrance of the holy name.

Knowledge and love are thus intimately wedded from the earliest days of biblical revelation until the end of time: "Everyone who loves is begotten of God and knows God" (1 Jn. 4:7). Love here is not a sentimental game according to our human way, but always an enlistment in a covenant sealed by three characteristics: the knowledge of the name, its historical manifestation through the realization of a promise which is initiated by God, and a commandment that sets us on our way toward Him.

It is under these specific and significant conditions that the name reveals itself in each of the great stages of revelation. In the covenant with Noah (Gen. 9:1–17), God reveals Himself under the name of Elohim; He promises him the fertility of the land and sovereignty over all that exists; He commands him not to kill. In the covenant with Abraham (Gen. 17), God gives Himself the name of El Shaddai (the One of the Mountain); He promises him numerous descendants as well as the land of Canaan. The commandment here is circumcision in which the body itself becomes the place of the covenant. Finally, in the covenant with Moses (Ex. 19 and following), God reveals the name of Yahweh, promises the land of Canaan and to be "the" God of "His" people (Ex. 6:7); He asks for obedience to the Law which, interiorized, offers us the experience of the divine presence.

At this stage, the divine name is, for the Jew, an invitation to an intimate dialogue in the face-to-face experience of prayer (Ex. 3:9-15) and a call to the highest requirements of sainthood (Ex. 6:2–9). This same name also involves the political undertakings of the whole nation which will endlessly invoke all that Yahweh has done for Israel (Ex. 33:12–34). Always, whether it be in the intimacy of his heart or in his many battles, the Jew depends on the name which for him means strength, sovereign power, deliverance from evil, and sometimes punishment. Yahweh Himself constantly points to the significance of His name: "See now that I, even I, am He, and there is no god beside Me; I kill and I make alive; I wound and I heal" (Deut. 32:39–40). And He solicits our response of faith: "O great and mighty God whose name is the Lord of hosts, great in counsel and mighty in deed; whose eyes are open to all the ways of men, rewarding every man according to his ways and according to the fruit of his doings" (Jer. 32:18–19). He also solicits our gratitude: "Yahweh has delivered me from all despair" (2 Sam. 4:9).

The holy name contains all the ways of God and all the faith of

23

Israel. Before this name "every knee shall bow," as the extraordinary prophecy of Isaiah states (Is. 45:23), and which the hymn to the Philippians will carry over to the name of Jesus. To sanctify this name, Israel will offer its life to God through an heroic loyalty which often ends in martyrdom (Phil. 2–10), and which will also be the fundamental attitude of the disciples from the very first days of the birth of Christianity: "These men who have risked their lives in the name of the Lord Jesus Christ" (Acts 15:26) and are "ready to die for the name of the Lord Jesus Christ" (Acts 21:13). In this, they do nothing other than that which Christ Himself does by giving His life on the cross to "glorify the name of the Father." "If any one serves Me, he must follow Me" (Jn. 12:26).

Only those who "serve Yahweh and love His name until death" (Is. 56:6) will know Him in that intimate reciprocity proper to lovers: "I will wed you to Me forever … I will lead you in justice and righteousness, in tenderness and mercy, in loyalty, and you will know Yahweh. You will call Me: 'my husband' … I will say: you are My people and you will say: My God" (Hosea 2:18–23). But this intimacy in the depths of the heart of each person radiates on all peoples who also become a holy people, "bearers of the name of Yahweh" (Deut. 48:9), belonging to Him, trustees of His glory and "praising the name all the days of their lives" (Ps. 34:1–5). That is the only aspiration of the saints of Yahweh.

We carry these great stages in the biblical journey toward the mystical wedding in the memory of our ancestral cells. Each one of us also relives them in our own spiritual growth, as our own personal Old Testament right through to the full revelation of the last and definitive covenant, when the name reveals its face in Jesus Christ, with the promise that we, too, will become the dwelling place of God. He, in turn, will become our dwelling place if the commandment of love is fulfilled.

 The Bible, therefore, describes our own itinerary in the discovery and knowledge of the name which always translates the essence of our faith, pointing to which God we believe in and how we believe in Him. Noah, Abraham and Moses are our prototypes, the steps of our interior ladder which we must climb. They are the signposts of our personal path, balancing our progress and giving us the right direction. Without pretension, we must be able to put our name in the place of all these biblical fi gures. The text then suddenly takes on a stunning coloration, so immediate and personal that it is a revelation for us today. The Spirit within leads us to understand to what extent the tradition is not a dead letter from an obscure past forever resolved, but a living reality which now anchors itself in us.

It is always the same eternity at the heart of passing time, always the same Presence under different faces, always the same revelation which gives meaning to the varied events of history. It is this name that God sends to speak in the concrete reality of our existence. When the Bible speaks of Noah, Abraham, Moses and all the others down to Revelation, it is always speaking of us: "You are the man," says the Prophet Nathan to David (2 Sam. 12:7). The mystery is infinite and our exploration of it never ends as we learn who we are in the eyes of God and what He is for each of us today.

The roots of our invocation of the holy name of Jesus are found there, in the hearts of the patriarchs, of the prophets, and in the assembly of the people. For the Hebrews, the invocation is first of all intrinsically linked to the places of worship, to such an extent that they called them "sanctuaries," because that is where the name was sanctified and where it was manifested. Always, "from encampment to encampment," Abraham built an altar to Yahweh to invoke His name (Gen. 12:8–9).

Later, Yahweh Himself will initiate the location of His dwelling, that rallying point for all the tribes of Israel. "It is only in the place chosen by Yahweh your God, among all your tribes, that you will come to find it" (Deut. 12:5). This was so often repeated that building a sanctuary or going to the sanctuary was synonymous with invoking the name of the Lord. But if the sanctuary offers a dwelling place for the name, it is only at the heart of the dialogue between God and humanity which occurs where it reveals itself, a dialogue in which invocation is done according to the conditions of our life: supplication (Ps. 124:8; Chron. 5:20), confident prayer (Ps. 20:8), thanksgiving (Ps. 63:5), jubilation (Ps. 20:6; Ps. 89:13), benediction (Ps. 129:8). The holy name is celebrated in all its tonalities: blessing

(Ps. 96:2), celebrating (Ps. 44:9), singing (Ps. 69:31), exalting and magnifying (Ps. 34:4), playing and dancing for Him (Ps. 7:18; 2 Sam. 6:16). These few citations among so many seem empty and tedious listed in such a way, but for the person who will meditate on them, each one evokes a concrete experience of the presence of God through the most varied situations in which the name is invoked.

To name God at the heart of an event is to give that event its true face, to transfigure it and to imprint a new orientation on it, according to the divine will acting at the heart of everything. "To invoke," from the Hebrew *gara*, means "to name," which in the Semitic mentality means to call into existence, to create: "God calls light day ... God calls the firmament sky ..." (Gen. 1). An event, a circumstance are dead letters until they are named by their true name, the name which gives them life. The one who names with that faith lifts the veil from appearances and makes possible an encounter in every moment with the depths of things. In that act, God Himself gives a name to humanity and when, beyond their ordinary names, He names Abraham (Gen. 17:5), Sara (Gen. 17:15) or Jacob (Gen. 32:29), as Jesus will later do for some of His disciples, it is a creative act that regenerates the heart toward a new destiny.

Life thus perceived becomes the sanctuary of the name and the place of the covenant forever deepened, betrayed and renewed. As a constant reminder of this reality, the Ark, which was identified by the name of Yahweh, was always present (Num. 10:35) among the people, carried on their shoulders during the long march toward the Promised Land or placed at the center of the most brutal battles (1 Sam. 4). The pious Jew who does not live at this level of history, forcing himself to read it in a way that leads him beyond it toward its mystery, falls, like every person, into a search which is not for the name but for worldly ambition. To escape the worst, he begs the Lord: "Not to us, Yahweh, not for us, but in Your name give glory" (Ps. 115:1). The invocation becomes the impetus for the heart and its prayer. "I call upon you, Yahweh, all the day" (Ps. 88:10). "I have found He whom my heart loves, I have seized Him and will not let Him go" (Song 3:4).

The foundational event of history is announced in the burning bush, but the question which Moses asks of God: "What is Your name?" receives only a temporary response. Thus, the prayer of Israel with that of all peoples, though more unconsciously, is an immense waiting. The promise that filled with hope every invocation of the name down through the centuries, will realize itself on the "Day of Yahweh," announced by all the prophets in the fullness of the last days when salvation will be offered to "all who call upon the name of the Lord" (Joel 2:32). This day is Pentecost, the true origin of a new humanity to which the holy name will reveal its definitive identity and show its face at the heart of an experience of fire, as was witnessed in the great theophanies of the Old Testament.

To show that it is, indeed, its historical fulfillment and recapitulation,

St. Peter, entrusted with the task of explaining the decisive event to the crowd, chooses the prophecy of Joel which best synthesizes the very essence of the Jewish tradition: "And in the last days it shall be, God declares … whoever calls on the name of the Lord shall be saved" (Acts 2:17–21).

But what is this "great day," this "name," this "Lord" and this "salvation"? Peter, filled with the fullness of the Spirit, at the risk of his life, affirms with power before the stupefied Jews and the Apostles drunk with joy: "It is Jesus of Nazareth!" This revelation of the name in the grandiose framework of Pentecost makes of this event a new Horeb, a definitive response to the question of Moses and of all people, which opens "the great day" wherein Yahweh mysteriously reveals in Jesus His own face (Jn. 14:9) and sends us the unique "Lord" without whom there is no "salvation."

All the prophecies are fulfilled in Jesus who unifies them, gives them meaning and carries them, in ways unimaginable, beyond themselves. "Let all the house of Israel, therefore, know assuredly that God has made Him both Lord and Christ, this Jesus whom you crucified … And there is salvation in no one else, for there is no other name under heaven given among men by which we must be saved" (Acts 2:36; 4:12). "To invoke the name" has henceforth its fulfillment only in faith in the Lord Jesus, and the name of Jesus now substitutes for the holy name of Yahweh: "It is the name that I will bear forever, under which future generations will invoke Me" (Ex. 3:15). The glory of the

holy name of Yahweh promised and partially manifested throughout the Old Testament becomes full sacrament in the name of Jesus: "God has given Him the name which is above every name" (Phil. 2:9).

In the thinking of the true Jew, one must, indeed, pick up the stones which will destroy this blasphemy. Peter will go to prison and will have to justify himself before the Sanhedrin. The other disciples will follow Him, "hated by all and persecuted because of the name" (Mt. 5:11; Jn. 15:21; Mk. 13:13). For centuries, generations of Christians will go to martyrdom, "suffering for the name, without tiring" (Rev. 2:3). To say that Jesus is Lord and to ask to be baptized in His name led them straight to death.

Today, we can no longer fully understand the enthusiasm of the fi rst Christians and the immensity of the scandal which they created among the Jews. For them, the holy name of Yahweh had become so fearsome (Deut. 28:58) that, by a quivering respect before the transcendence of the inaccessible and mysterious God, no one dared to pronounce it. The high priest alone would have that right, once a year, at the feast of Expiation, in the Holy of Holies of the temple. The name of Yahweh would be replaced by Adonai or Elohim, and when the Bible is translated into Greek, Yahweh is systematically translated as Kyrios, Lord, which then becomes the name of God and itself becomes a mysterious name, "bearer of a secret" and designating, as the name of Yahweh Himself, the person of the revealed and incommunicable God.

Under the power of the Spirit, which alone gives the grace of a right invocation, the first Christians carry over without hesitation the name of Kyrios upon Jesus of Nazareth, whom God has made Lord, "Lord of all" (Acts 10:36): Jesus is indeed God!

For them, it is by this name of "Lord Jesus Christ" that all the prophecies are fulfilled. Baptized in the name, those who invoke it in repentance and under the movement of the Spirit enter into the messianic community which represents hereafter the "little remnant" of Israel, the "holy remnant" and the prophecies of universal salvation of which the Church will become the bearer (Acts 2:38–47). This consciousness is so ardent among the first Christians that they are called "those who invoke the name of the Lord" (Acts 3:14; 1 Cor. 1:2). That was "their" work, for they invoked it not only in worship and prayer, but through every activity (Col. 3:17). Finally, it was their way of being, the Christian life itself, that of the "assembly of the firstborn" (Heb. 12:23). Nothing was done with any other motive than doing it "in the name of the Lord."

This was a constant and radical conversion to the resurrected Christ through the invocation of His name which opened not only the heart but every event to His presence and could hurry the final return

(Thess. 1:9–10). The invocation of the name of Yahweh was fulfilled in the very incarnation of that name, the glory of Yahweh manifested in the midst of His people (Jn. 12:28; 17:1), the sacrament of the invisible God. To invoke the name of the Lord was to invoke Yahweh: whoever knows the Son knows the Father (Jn. 14:9). This transparency is the work of the Spirit. No one can invoke the Father without the Spirit (Ps. 8:15) and no one can say of Jesus that He is Lord without that same Spirit (1 Cor. 12:3).

The invocation of the name of Jesus, therefore, introduces Christians into the mystery of the divine Trinity, itself the source of the messianic community and the inspiration to the whole life of the baptized. One name in three Persons. It is the backdrop behind the invocation of the name of Jesus, the revelation of the Father and of the Spirit. That is why the name is love. "I am the One who will be" (Ex. 3:14) is the secret given to Moses in which God inscribes His name in a future which will only fully reveal its meaning on the cross. There, in this utter giving up of self for humanity, God spells out to us His name, for "there is no greater love than to give one's life" (Jn. 15).

The name of Jesus is the glory of all this mystery, the origin and end of all, the "Alpha and Omega." Through this name, the Apostles not only do all sorts of miracles (Mt. 7:22; Acts 4:30), healing the sick (Acts 3:6; 9:34) and chasing out demons (Mk. 9:37; Lk. 10:17), but the whole of life is impregnated by one unique motive: living in the name of the Lord. They come together in His name (Mt. 18:20); they receive others because of His name (Eph. 5:20); "in all times and in every way they render thanks to God in the name of Jesus Christ" (Mt. 5:3–12); "we suffer because of Him and are happy because of Him" (2 Thess. 1:12); every attitude must "glorify the name of our Lord Jesus Christ" (Col. 3:17) "whatever you do or say . . . " (Acts 4:7–12). Lived, in such a way the fabric of life itself is eternal salvation (Mt. 1:21) and the meaning of the name of Jesus — "Yahweh saves" — is the dynamism of the present moment. That is where is found the unique goal of every testimonial (Lk. 24:46) and the only wealth of the Church (Acts 3:6). This is the ultimate revelation of the "secret" through Jesus: the name is a life and a way of living. "In that day you will ask nothing of Me. Truly, truly, I say to you, if you ask anything of the Father, He will give it to you in My name. Hitherto you have asked nothing in My name; ask, and you will receive, that your joy may be full" (Jn. 16:23–24). The name of Jesus, therefore, reveals to us the ways of God and His fatherly tenderness.

Chapter Two

THE JESUS PRAYER
IN THE EARLY TRADITION

Find the door of your heart and you will discover paradise.

St. John Chrysostom

After the New Testament, no one passes on the torch of this witness better than the martyr, for he enters into the full revelation of the treasure. The martyr puts us in contact with the burning love of the earliest times. "To vow one's life to the name and to die for Him" (Acts 15:26; 21:13), such was the ideal lived with great passion in the primitive Church and such is still and forever the basis of every Christian life, even if history has sometimes forgotten it. One can only answer to the revelation of the name through the cross with the gift of one's blood for the loved One. The measure of love is to be without measure, say the Fathers. Any less and there is no true knowledge of one another, only rote calling on the name, not eternal life (Jn. 17:3).

To live, for the Christian, is to enter daily into the arena of this

35

combat, suffering everything for the sake of the name (Col. 1:29; Rev. 2:3) and resisting "to the blood" all that separates us from it (Heb. 12:4). "No one lives for himself ..."; "If we live, we live for the Lord, and if we die, we die for the Lord" (Rom. 14:7).

 The Spirit acted with power and inscribed with letters of fi re the invocation of the sacred name on the hearts of the faithful. How could it be otherwise, since the Lord Himself required it? "Until now, you asked nothing in My name; ask and you shall receive!" (Jn. 16:24). One need only read the letters of St. Ignatius of Antioch in the year 110 under the Emperor Trajan), a disciple of John, to understand what wild love the first Christians attached to the name of Jesus! A limitless tenderness, far from all sentimentality, virile and heroic: "Never has man written like this man, for none of those who have written have ever loved like him!" (Hausherr, Names of Christ, p. 37.)

It is in this soil that we must plunge our roots and satisfy our thirst, otherwise we will not know what it means truly to be a disciple of Christ or what joy is promised to us as of now and at the very heart of the thousand sufferings and deaths which the world thrusts upon us.

Chained to ten leopards, mistreated by guards, dragged from Antioch to Rome to be thrown to the beasts, Ignatius transcribed with words of fire the passion that animated him: "May nothing visible or invisible keep me from attaining Christ. May all the torments of the devil fall upon me, as long as I attain Christ. It is more glorious for me to die for Christ than to reign over the whole world. It is He I search, this Jesus who has died for us. It is He I want, the one who is resurrected because of us. Here is the moment in which I will begin to live" (Letter to the Romans). "Nothing escapes the Lord, our very secrets are in His hands. Let us then in all our actions think that He lives within us, so that we may be His temple and that He, our God, may be in us" (Letter to the Ephesians).

It is important to breathe the atmosphere of the apostolic times. It is no longer ours, unfortunately, and that is why we breathe so poorly and do not live correctly. Without pronouncing the name each time that they spoke of it, these Christians were so fi lled with it that, in fact, they lived and died only by and for the name! Th is total offering to the name, through love, is a martyrdom, whether it leads to the shedding of blood or not, a "Gnostic martyrdom," says Clement of Alexandria in the year 193, "because Gnosis is the knowledge of the name."

For centuries to come, it was in this ambiance that marvelous texts were written on the name and its invocation which were expressions of a new consciousness of life. One of the first to evoke it was Hermas (around 150): "All who have once suffered for the name are glorious to God ... The name of the Son of God is great, infinite, and upholds the whole world ... To receive the name of the Son of God is to escape death and to give oneself to life ... No one can enter into the kingdom if it is not through the name of the Son ..." Each of these sentences is weighty with contemplation and charged with an experience in which the name contains the entire Christian mystery. They are not created merely to be read, but to nourish us.

At the end of the second century, one of the greatest geniuses of humanity, Origen (d. 253), who cannot be underestimated as a scholar, and whose teaching has never ceased to fascinate seekers, writes: "I would like to carry the name of Christ; I would like to carry this name which is a benediction to the earth. This is my desire: that my spirit as my works gives me the right to have this name." He adds: "Today again the name of Jesus appeases troubled souls, overcomes demons, heals the sick; its use infuses a kind of wonderful gentleness; it assures the purity of our ways; it inspires humanity with generosity." This prodigious fervor for Jesus is found everywhere in Origen's work. He never ceases to call Him: "My Lord Jesus ... My Jesus."

One of the most exceptional singers of the name is St. Ephrem the Syrian (d. 373). His talent as a poet overflows with a passionate lyricism: "Jesus, name worthy of praise, invisible bridge that leads from death to life. To You have I arrived, and there is no further to go."

Our goal here is not to exhaust this immense outpouring which clearly shows that it is the same faith found in the Acts of the Apostles which continues to make its way down through the centuries. What is important is not so much the scholarship as the need to quench our thirst for prayer today at the source of the masters of yesterday. For them, the power of God is truly present in the name of Jesus. The invocation acts in the manner of a sacrament with divinizing power.

This river of worship and of love for the name also spread in the west, from the earliest times right through to the French School, home of a spiritual current during the seventeenth century. Certain pearls deserve to be acclaimed. Saint Paulinus of Nola (bishop in the fifth century) writes: "This name is a nectar to the mouth, honey; it is a splendid ambrosia; if one has tasted it, he will never let it go; it is to the eyes a serene light, to the ears the very sound of life."

Saint Caesarius of Arles (d. 542) emotionally evokes the "blessed name" as does St. Augustine (d. 430) who says: "The name is so friendly and so sweet to pronounce." One only needs to invoke it, says St. Athanasius (d. 373), and the demons scurry off. "Who is this Savior that I cry out His name? It is Jesus. Jesus forgets the vain one who has provoked Him, looks at the unhappy one who invokes the gentle name, the delectable name, the name which comforts the sinner, the name of happy hope. I glorify myself in You, in the midst of all who love Your name," cries out St. Anselm (d. 1109).

A new tonality begins in this period, to which St. Bernard (d. 1153) brings such vigor that he creates an entire literature around the name. "The name of Jesus is like diffused oil; it shines when we proclaim it, it nourishes us when we meditate upon it, it appeases and penetrates when we invoke it." Thomas of Celano describes how St. Francis of Assisi (d. 1226) relished the name of Jesus and was "captivated" by its very sound: "As soon as you hear His name, you should adore the Lord with respect and fear, prostrated on the ground." Saint Francis carries the name of Jesus in his heart, on his lips, in his ears, on his tongue, in his hands, in all his members; and when he pronounces it, he is seized by an emotion which reason cannot comprehend, and he seems a new man in a new time.

With the Franciscan movement, the veneration of the name of Jesus became popular and widespread. The brothers counseled the faithful to call upon the holy name of Jesus in order to obtain, for example, deliverance from demonic temptations. Henry Suso (d. 1366) goes so far as to carve the name on his chest, seeking a "fusion" through continual prayer, and associating the Lord with the slightest beating of his heart. The emblem "I.H.S." was sewn on garments, liturgical ornaments, then painted or sculpted on church walls, monuments, homes, imprinted on letters and even carved on money. Joan of Arc inscribed the names of Jesus and of Mary on her flag; on the stake at Orleans, her last words would be a single, endlessly repeated word:

"Jesus … Jesus …"

Around the name of Jesus are also born all sorts of brotherhoods and societies, bringing forth abundant publications and masses glorifying the holy name, culminating in the advent of the "Society of Jesus." The brotherhoods often had as a goal to teach those who were condemned to death the invocation of the name of Jesus as preparation for their journey. The name of Jesus became for the people an experience of light and a source of grace.

But this popular fervor fizzled out in the last centuries; in the west, education no longer nourished it and only a few saints maintained it. If it is true that they are often heralds of new times and beacons for the future, then we can undoubtedly have great hope, because Charles de Foucauld (d. 1916) and St. Thérèse of Lisieux (d. 1897), at the dawn of our century, were fascinated by the name of Jesus, repeating it endlessly, seeing "their unique treasure" everywhere, and naming themselves with the name: Charles of Jesus, Theresa of the Child Jesus.

 This great love for the divine name became the ground in which would grow the seed of every prayer called "the Jesus Prayer" or "the Prayer of the Heart."

As we have seen, the profound reality of the Prayer of the Heart was powerfully present during the whole Judeo-Christian tradition from the origins of the Old Testament. It enlivened the faith of entire peoples and raised up giants of holiness.

The invocation of the name could take on many forms in the Old Testament: "Spare Thy people, O Lord" (Joel 2:17); "O Lord, I beseech Thee, Save my life!" (Ps. 116:4); "The Lord, the Lord, a God merciful and gracious!" (Ex. 34:6); "Save me, O God, by Thy name!" (Ps. 54:1) or simply the repetition of the name "Adonai" as later the name "Jesus" would be repeated. In the New Testament, we find the cry of the blind men on the roadside: "Have mercy on us, Son of David" (Mt. 10:27); or the cry of the publican: "God, be merciful to me a sinner!" (Lk. 18:13). These cries are distant forerunners of the Jesus Prayer.

But it would take many more centuries to see it formulated in its current phrasing. A slow maturation of the spiritual consciousness is necessary to bring together in so few words the essence of the Christian faith and to offer us the arrow capable of making its way into our hearts.

1. The Birth of the Prayer of the Heart

The first to introduce a systemization of the prayer seems to be John Cassian, author of a veritable Philokalia of the Desert Fathers, which appeared in 399. The words which he repeats again and again are taken from the first verse of Psalm 70: "Be pleased, O God, to deliver me! O Lord, make haste to help me!" As will later be said of the Jesus Prayer, this pondering awakens pity within us; makes us conquer all temptations; fights all illnesses of the soul; bad inclinations, vices, especially of the flesh, irritations, dangers and occasions of sin. It battles all illusions, the nocturnal manifestation of demons, and helps to maintain the perpetual remembrance of God. Soon this repetition leads to a "perfection of prayer without images" and is eventually no longer expressed with words; it becomes an outburst of fire, an ineffable rapture, an insatiable impetuosity of spirit. Ravished out of the senses and out of all things visible, it is through groans and sighs that the soul overflows toward God.

Saint Anthony the Great (fourth century), the "father of monasticism," also used the short expressin and counseled the continual "pondering" of a sentence from Scripture. Saint Arsenius (fourth century), champion of hesychasm (from the Greek hesychia: repose, quiet, tranquillity; it is a way of life in silence and interior peace sought by those who practice constant prayer). He would say over and over: "Lord, lead me in such a way that I may be saved," or "God, do not abandon me." Saint Macarius entered into the same movement: "The Lord knows all that is useful to us, one only needs to cry out" — "Lord, help me!" or in an attitude of surrender: "May Your will be done, Lord, as it pleases You!"

Lucius, monk of Antioch, repeated incessantly the first verse of Psalm 51: "Have mercy on me, O God, according to Thy steadfast love!"

Whether explicitly admitted in prayer or not, the important effort for everyone was to be freed from that obstacle on the way: sin. That is why St. Nil (fifteenth century Russian monk) would say that on must fight the demons through "the remembrance of our Savior, the fervent invocation of the venerable name day and night, the rumination on inspired words" and by "throwing oneself before God crying: Son of God, save me."

Saint John Chrysostom interprets the injunction of Christ as an invitation to "a mental sobriety," for it is this which we must accomplish, not merely the mouthing of a multitude of words or the repeating of prayers by rote in the manner of the pagans. Christ teaches us a way of prayer and commands us, as does St. Paul, to make short and frequent prayers at small intervals. "In doing this, it will be easy for you to remain awake and you will say your prayers with great presence of spirit."

2. Mount Sinai

Not far from the deserts of Egypt and Palestine, where most of those whom we have cited lived, came the first witness of the Sinai movement: St. Diadochus of Photike (fifth-century Greek). The fatherhood of the Jesus Prayer is often attributed to him, but in fact, he never uses the classic expression. It is the perpetual remembrance of God that he emphasizes and which is, of course, the backdrop of the Jesus Prayer. The sin of disobedience, he tells us, has thrown man, simple and unified at the beginning, into a schizophrenic rupture and makes of the soul a home of many psychic passions. One must, then, through the constant remembrance of God, act upon the memory to recover that lost unity. The way to accomplish this is to "meditate on the glorious and holy name in the depths of the heart with great attention and care" so that, little by little, every thought disappears; the memory then becomes unified, and original simplicity enters our consciousness. But this is impossible without asceticism which is, for Diadochus, the "firm decision of man to turn himself entirely toward God." Asceticism is also understood as a daily exercise or combat to let the grace of God penetrate us. It is only in this "resolute effort, a disposition of humility, practicing the commandments, and calling endlessly on the Lord, that the fire of holy grace will illuminate our senses." Grace is a gift of God, the manifestation and communication of His energies.

Saint John Climacus (d. 649), famous for his book *The Holy Ladder*, which inspired generations of monks, is the one around whom the whole Sinaite spirituality crystallized. He tells us that we must banish reflection, ignore our many thoughts when in prayer and attach ourselves to one single word in order to enter into "complete unconcern for all things because a single hair suffices to blur our vision, a single worry to destroy the hesychia. Solitude is the stripping of thoughts and the renouncing of all worries." "Through the name of Jesus, whip your enemies, for there is not in heaven or earth as powerful a weapon." "May the remembrance of Jesus be one with your breathing, then you will know the usefulness of hesychia which is perpetual adoration in the presence of God." The name of Jesus must then "glue itself" to our breath so that it may communicate its energy and its grace to us. Contemplation then bears its fruit and becomes a communion beyond all discourse. Since rational thought and the imagination especially are the instigators of our actions, the "control of thought" and the "watch over the heart" through the Prayer of the Name will remodel us both in our interior depths and in our exterior activities.

With *The Centuries of Hesychius*, written by Hegumen de Bates at Mount Sinai in the eighth century, and which is one of the most important documents on the hesychast prayer, we move a step further: Not only must the Jesus Prayer (he is the first to use this expression) "be continually breathed in, and unite itself to our breathing, but it must unite itself to our whole life. When the spirit is purified and unified through prayer, our thoughts swim within it like happy dolphins in a calm sea. Then a dialogue begins in which Christ, who has become the interior Master, makes known His will to the heart. The name of Jesus enters into our life first like a lamp in the darkness, then it takes on the glimmer of moonlight, finally it becomes the rising sun." The sun, obviously, enlightens all things and all life depends on it. The Jesus Prayer, for Hesychius, is all-consuming and fills our whole existence, whatever we do, whether we pray or work, in the same way that we must breathe continuously.

3. St. Symeon the New Theologian (949–1022)

Here is certainly the greatest name known to Orthodox spirituality
after the Patristic period, alongside St. Gregory Palamas, monk of
Mount Athos, then Bishop of Thessalonica in the fourteenth century.
Symeon emphasized the priority of the spiritual and the necessity of
the mystical experience as experiential knowledge of eternal life
beginning here and now. Symeon has been called the " lover" of
Christ and the "herald" of the Holy Spirit. He is literally possessed by
them.

Without speaking specifically of the Jesus Prayer as such, Symeon
nevertheless developed a very realistic spirituality of incorporation
in Christ, even on the physiological level: "The Spirit makes Christ
penetrate us to the ends of our fingers; He enters our bodies." Again,
in his Hymns, he writes: "I, unworthy, am the hand and the foot of
Christ! I move my hand and my hand is all Christ, for the divinity of
God has united itself indivisibly to me." Here, the spiritual return of
our being goes as far as a psychosomatic mutation that changes the
entire human condition. But Symeon is part of an already ancient
tradition, for St. Macarius preached in the fi fth century: "How can
one have eyes that are not His, or ears, hands, and feet that are not
His?"

For many years, a famous work entitled Method of Prayer and
Sacred Attention was attributed to Symeon. But the exegetes, in

particular I. Hausherr, who published a critical edition of the text, have shown that the author was probably the monk Nicephorus who lived at Mount Athos in the fourteenth century and was one of the masters of Gregory Palamas. Nicephorus himself merely restructured ancient practices that go back beyond the Sinaites. The "Method" consists of sitting in darkness, lowering the head, staring at the middle of the torso to discover the place of the heart, and repeating tirelessly *"Lord Jesus Christ, Son of God, have pity on me!"* This is done in rhythm with one's breathing, which is slowed as much as possible, and excludes all discursive thought. "The perseverance day and night of this practice opens the heart and gives love, joy, peace and all the rest; every desire is transformed."

In this context, we must cite a monk named Chrysostom, who left us this magnificent text: "We must repeat from morning till night: 'Lord Jesus, Son of God, have pity on us.' We must pray thus when eating and drinking. We must remember Jesus Christ until the name of the Lord penetrates our heart, descends deeply into it, crushes the dragon and vivifies the soul. Our heart must absorb the Lord, and the Lord must absorb our heart so that both may become one."

4. Mount Athos (14th–15th Century)

The Jesus Prayer had existed for a long time on Mount Athos when Gregory Palamas, leaving Sinai, arrived on that holy mountain. But it is through him that it recovered all its power. During this period, the rigidity of the expression and the mind- body technique were insisted upon. Saint Gregory said that one must hold as close as possible to a single expression, for plants that are too often transplanted do not take root. Prayer gives birth within us to a mystical life which, for Gregory, is the awakening of the energy of the Spirit latent in us since our baptism. It is not a matter of repeating the name of Jesus mechanically, but of nourishing ourselves with it as with food. It is a eucharistic communion which leads us to say with St. Paul: "It is not I who lives but Christ who lives in me," or according to the cry of St. Gregory himself: "Flesh of my flesh, bones of my bones." We are called to a deification in our totality body- soul- spirit, and the invocation of the name brings us to the vision of the light of Tabor that emanated from Christ during His transfiguration on Mount Tabor (Lk. 9:28).

This theology led to a hateful polemic between Greeks and Latins, sparked by the monk Barlaam, an adversary of Gregory Palamas and the Hesychasts. Saint Gregory pointed out in that period the famous distinction between the inaccessible essence of God and the uncreated divine energies through which we experience God who gives Himself to those who invoke Him with faith and love. In 1355, the Orthodox Church declared this doctrine to be the official one. In St. Gregory's entourage on Mount Athos, the name of St. Maximus (a Greek monk and theologian of the seventh century) must be lifted up for having written that there was no better way of saying the Jesus Prayer than to let Mary say it within us. In forming the prayer in our depths, Mary forms Christ within us.

In this same period, we find the Centuries of Callistus and Ignatius Xanthopoulos (fourteenth-century monks from Mount Athos) who made of the Jesus Prayer a way of life. The prayer takes root in the respiratory movement and reaches right into the intimacy of being where it will find, according to the Song of Songs, its "wound of love." But its sign of authenticity must be faith and good works and its ascetic context must be silence, fasting, the study of Scripture and the Eucharist. The prayer induces a new style of life — the hesychast life.

5. The Philokalia and The Way of the Pilgrim (18th Century)

The eighteenth century is marked, in the West, by the publication of the Encyclopedia which brought together all human knowledge and represents a triumph of rationalism. At the same time in the East, Mount Athos, after a period of decline, awakened and published in 1782 the *Philokalia,* a great work compiling all the hesychast knowledge. It represents a triumph of the "person hidden in the heart" and of the uncreated light which comes to flood us with the Trinitarian presence.

Philokalia means "love of beauty"; it is the work of St. Macarius of Corinth (1731–1805) and of St. Nicodemus the Hagiorite (1748–1809). These writings are a summation of the hesychast life and especially of the Jesus Prayer. "This book," says Nicodemus, "is the treasure of sobriety, the safeguard of intelligence, the mystic teaching of the prayer of the spirit, the eminent model of the active life, the infallible guide of contemplation, the paradise of the Fathers and the chain of virtues. A book which teaches the intimate remembrance of Jesus."

Besides this vast anthology of the hesychast prayer, St. Nicodemus wrote other works, particularly on the Jesus Prayer, in which he takes up the teaching of the Fathers on the way of sitting and the retention of breath to avoid dispersion, and in which he counsels its practice in the evening for one or two hours without interruption in a calm and dark place. He emphasizes that it is not a matter of mechanical repetition but of the seizing of the human being in his or her totality, without which the prayer alone cannot do its work: "We must put in action the power of the will, the soul must say the prayer with all its will, strength and love, without image or form."

Parallel to this movement of renewal on Mount Athos, the Jesus Prayer finds its apostle in the Slavonic countries, with Starets Paisius Velichkovsky (1722–1794). His translation of the Philokalia into Slavonic had an immense influence on the Russian people in all levels of society, from the intellectual aristocracy to the simple peasant. Out of these charismatic currents were born great Russian startsy (spiritual teachers), such as St. Seraphim of Sarov, and spiritual works such as *The Way of the Pilgrim*.

Saint Seraphim (d. 1833) is as popular in Russia as St. Francis is in the West. Seraphim was literally transfigured by the Taboric light, radiated with the Paschal joy, and was truly possessed by God. "All science is there: going or coming, sitting or standing, at work, at church, let the Jesus Prayer constantly flow from your lips — "Lord Jesus Christ, have mercy on me, a sinner." With this prayer in the heart, you will find interior peace and sobriety of body and of the soul.

"When you begin to pray, bring together all the interior forces of your spirit, join them to your heart and remain attentive. For one or two days make the prayer only with your spirit by pronouncing attentively and separately each word. When the Lord warms your heart by His grace and brings together all your energies in a single thought, the interior prayer will become for you a source of living waters that run endlessly, nourishing you, vivifying you constantly... When the soul is purified by penitence, then man, in proportion to his zeal and attachment of his spirit to his loved One, finds in the invocation of the name delights which awaken in him the will to seek the highest illumination."

Seraphim is the living witness of this phenomenon. His extraordinary power of radiance came from the total stripping of himself so that he became transparent to God: "Like the iron which abandons itself to the blacksmith, I have entirely surrendered myself to God and it is He alone who acts within me."

The Way of the Pilgrim, written by an anonymous author, appeared in 1884 in Kazan, a Russian town. The narrative tells of how a starets submits the pilgrim to a progressive training: he must say the prayer three thousand times a day, then six thousand and finally twelve thousand times. Then, ceasing to count, his prayer associates itself with his breathing and with each beat of his heart. One day his lips are quieted, he only listens to his heart, and the prayer nourishes him when he is hungry, quenches his thirst, gives him rest when he is tired, protects him from dangers and despair, and inspires him in each moment. "Sometimes my heart bursts with joy at being so light and full of liberty ... Sometimes I felt a burning love toward Jesus Christ ... Sometimes, invoking the name of Jesus, I was overwhelmed with happiness ..."

This little book is a pearl of Orthodoxy, an evangelical jewel in the midst of our barbaric times; it is to be read by all who would practice the Jesus Prayer!

6. Modern Times

Two great names arise at the dawn of the nineteenth century, both bishops retiring into the solitary life after years of ministry: St. Ignatius Brianchaninov (1807–1867) and St. Theophan the Recluse (1815–1894). Ignatius and Theophan both translated the Philokalia.

Theophan's translation, which considerably amplified the text, left aside the mind- body technique which, according to him, "scandalizes some, alienates others from the practice, and deforms the exercise itself ... These processes are only exterior preparations to an interior activity, crutches ... To attach one's hope, if only by a single hair to some personal work, is already to turn away from the right path ... Make efforts to exhaustion, stretch your strength to its last degree, but await the actual work of salvation from the Lord alone."

In their work, they have taken up the ancient tradition and submitted it to a rigorous theological reflection. Being careful not to fall into quietism, they emphasize the feeling of sin and the gratuity of grace which is never a result of our ascetic efforts alone, even though nothing can be received without them. "The essence of the practice of the Jesus Prayer," says Theophan, "consists of acquiring the habit of remaining with the intellect in the heart, without images, in the conviction that God is near, that He sees and listens."

Ignatius and Theophan point to three stages in the Jesus Prayer: it is "difficult" at first because of the effort of will which involves the complete gift of self. When the answer of grace comes, the prayer becomes spontaneous. Finally, when words are no longer spoken, the prayer leads us into contemplation.

For Theophan, it is a matter of a true re- creation in which "the hands of God have touched my being; then the intellect, the heart and the body are reunited to constitute a complete unity, in which they are immersed in God."

Theophan insists, as no other teacher does, on the "feeling" of the presence. Because of the inseparable co-penetration of body- soul-spirit, he knows that, for human beings, everything goes through the body. The contrary could only be doubtful in a religion of incarnation. If Theophan has a critical attitude toward the mind-body methods, it is because of the "spiritualist" movements of his time and of the ever-present risk of a mechanical utilization of these processes which seek results at the end of our voluntary efforts. This justifiable suspicion did not stop him from taking up for himself the counsels of the Fathers on the hesychast method of sitting and breathing, the physical union of the intellect and the heart, the warmth felt in the chest, the great importance of "feeling" through which "all religion begins."

History does not have enough objectivity yet to speak of our century. There are people steeped in prayer on the holy mountain of Athos, in Russia and in other parts of the world, forever buried in the silence of their caves and the catacombs of our times, true spiritual masters flooded by the divine light whose names we will never know. But they do not cease to nourish the world secretly without our knowing it, for we only subsist through the prayer of the saints.

Two of them, however, because they have left a teaching, are known to us: the saintly starets Silouan (b. 1838) and his disciple Father Sophrony. Sophrony lived until recently in a monastery he founded in England, where he shared the message received from Silouan. The

Two monks lived together on Mount Athos in a spiritual friendship that lasted twenty-one years. Christ came to Silouan in an experience of hellish darkness, in the depths of despair and abandonment, and the word God spoke to him became the light of his whole life and work: "Hold your soul in hell and do not despair!"

This light also burns in the darkness of our age of general despair where people, far from all repentance, and more lost than ever, no longer believe in the Resurrection. It is this more or less conscious self-condemnation to nothingness that fills the contemporary soul with melancholy. But "do not despair," Christ says to Silouan, for at the edge of this abyss is the Lord with all the immensity of His love for us.

This consciousness is precisely the place where all prayer takes root and makes possible the path toward the light. The acceptance of our hell — and we each have our own — living fully what is given to us to live here and now without despair, even in loving that which crucifies us, annihilates all passion in us and frees our heart to receive the divine love, to be more and more configured to Christ dead and resurrected: "Outside of this experience of descent into hell, it is impossible truly to know what is the love of Christ, His Golgotha and His Resurrection," writes Father Sophrony. It is "impossible," because that is where we find the foundation and the meaning of humility without which prayer is useless and even dangerous. When Silouan descended into the emptiness of his despair to the very doorstep of death, "Christ appeared to him with great power, the light of divinity illuminated him, and the grace of the Holy Spirit filled him fully, even his body; the uncreated life seized him and he put on the humility of Christ which is indescribable. Humility is the light in which we can see God."

When we pray in our hell, it is never in a superficial and external manner: we call toward God, sometimes with tears from the depths of our heart; then our intellect is united with our heart. Even if only for a brief moment, we can experience this rare reunification in us and know how to find it more often, thanks to our prayer. "The tears of compunction during prayer are a clear indication of the fusion of the intellect toward the heart, a sign that prayer has come to its proper place; that is why the ascetics hold tears in such high esteem." These are, of course, tears of repentance: we weep over our alienation from God and our suffering finds its cause in that separation.

Silouan was a man of prayer. The Jesus Prayer accompanied him day and night, and he showed us that this configuration to Jesus, which the prayer creates in the one who practices it, leads us on the same journey as Jesus took through suffering and death toward Resurrection here below. Jesus said: "I am the Way," and that there is no other way besides Him. "No one goes to the Father, but through Me" (Jn. 14:6). But if the Lord was transfigured, we also will be transfi gured now, on this earth, as long as our intimate aspirations are similar to His. On this path, there are many oases of light at the very heart of darkness. Path and prayer blend together, and because the path of that life is perpetual, so must be our prayer.

Chapter Three

THE PRACTICE OF THE JESUS PRAYER

When you pray, go into your room and shut the door and
pray to your Father who is in the secret place.
Matthew 6:6

The Jesus Prayer contains everything: the sky and the earth, humanity and God; it is the essence of all theology and anthropology, the very kernel of the Bible, a path of love in which humanity and God encounter each other, the place of intimate communion. Those who judged the hesychast monks in their day with the verdict of "navel gazers" could not have said it better! For in focusing on one's deepest center, we paradoxically escape from ourselves to attain the navel of the universe, the incandescent home of all life. It is to this focal point that life calls us at each moment, not merely once in a while. That is why the Jesus Prayer aims at becoming perpetual, and at conquering the fullness of time.

If it is true that only the prayer has the power to awaken and deepen the spirit within us, that which makes us human beyond the body and the soul, then only the one who prays is a normal human being. Because of this fact, prayer is above all things, before all things and must accompany them all. "Nothing good can be done without it," says the Russian pilgrim. The Jesus Prayer is precisely the practice which offers us this path for, the pilgrim says, "it is the continual and uninterrupted invocation of the name of Jesus on the lips, the heart and the mind, in the feeling of His presence, in all places, at all times, even during sleep: 'Lord Jesus Christ, Son of God, have mercy on me, a sinner!'"

Simple in the extreme, available to the poorest individual as well as to the greatest contemplative, this prayer leads us toward the penetration of the deepest mysteries. It makes us pilgrims on a journey toward our promised land — which is first of all our own heart — whether we are working in the fields or in the factory, at the office or cleaning house, doing our shopping at the supermarket, at the wheel of our car, whether stuck in our sick bed or in the best of health. There is no job or situation which cannot harmonize itself with it and which it does not illuminate with an entirely new light.

 Those who have chosen the Jesus Prayer as a pathway to life have no other interests — or rather all their other interests only find their meaning and their fulfillment in the prayer. Just as all who work at a great task are completely absorbed by it, so those who practice the prayer enclose themselves in Jesus, make Him their cloister and see and live everything else in and through Him. To such people we should be able to ask at any moment the question which Jesus asked His fi rst disciples: "What do you seek?" (Jn. 1:38), and they would infallibly answer, whatever their external task: "Jesus!" This absolute exclusivity, which alone achieves great works, unifies them; everything becomes simple because, for them, Jesus is the substance of all things, the "Truth and the Life" (Jn. 14:6), the answer to every problem, the fulfillment of all that is.

Constant interior prayer maintained in this consciousness never ceases to deepen and to transmute itself. This awareness of a bottomless present leads to the disappearance of thoughts, and especially of our multiple desires, the great symbol of the ego. Like oil, the holy name fills us with its presence.

As oil penetrates paper and makes it transparent, so we become transparent. An atmosphere is created within and around us. But as soon as we lose contact with this powerful feeling which is not an emotion, there is a lack. Everything becomes opaque, and we quickly become sleepwalkers again. This means that there is a real way of life in Christ, a way of being and of understanding all things in Him, of dealing with seemingly profane problems in this light. The Jesus Prayer leads us into such a contemplation.

At first, the prayer is pronounced with our lips, in a more or less rapid rhythm, but always putting our heart and mind into it, lovingly focusing our attention on God, each word of the prayer absorbing our whole consciousness.

At other times, according to external circumstances or if we are tired, it can be said between long intervals during which we simply taste this atmosphere of the presence which never leaves us, much like a bird beating its wings once and letting itself glide in an act of abandon. Just as that bird discovers that there is no void beneath it, so we, through the prayer, discover the presence which precedes and accompanies us, carries and ravishes us toward divine spheres; these spheres are not of the world and yet well within it, here and now. The name of Jesus is a revelation of new dimensions within and around us. In the Gospel, when the prayer was said by the blind — whom we are today — they received the light and saw, and the world revealed itself to them (Mt. 20:30–34 and Lk.18:38).

But unless the whole universe becomes light for us some day, we must begin, according to the invitation of Christ Himself, by descending into the crypt of our heart where the divine spark is found which, in solitude, can turn into fire.

One day, Abba Arsenius, a giant of the hesychasm of the earliest times, received from the Lord Himself this saying which became the basis of his whole prayer: "Run away, be still, maintain recollection." These are the three degrees of silence. At the beginning of the spiritual life, there is first a separation which strips us from all that is useless, offers us the indispensable conditions, and reorients our being. This separation is a physical necessity: we plunge into a solitude which alters everything radically. Once this physical space is opened, it also becomes an interior reality in which we can enter even in the midst of noise. It creates a state of the soul which is immune to all things and is indifferent to the solicitations of the world. In this interior retreat begins the true conquest of silence. This battle lasts a lifetime and leads to the suppression of all bad thoughts, for in them is found "the source and the principle of every sin," as Origen says. Each thought which presents itself is questioned: "Are you with us or against us?" and, depending on the response, it is either crushed or transfigured by the prayer. This is a rigorous asceticism without which there is neither prayer nor silence. This conviction is unanimous among the fathers who repeat it in many ways.

When the mental silence becomes effective, it produces recollection, a descent into the heart where silence becomes *the Stillness* which St. Ignatius of Antioch described as giving birth to Jesus Christ. With this silence is also born the Jesus Prayer within us. In this recollection, every person becomes a listener, and this is the great method which the Bible proposes: "Shema Israel — Listen O Israel!" — an attitude which contains the three characteristics of silence: "Run away, be still, maintain recollection" in a continual progress toward a silence- virginity and a silence-fertility. It is only when we are in complete silence like Him that the Father can engender the word within us and that we can hear it: "This is my beloved Son, listen to Him!" (Lk. 9:35). And He descends into "the crypt of our heart" as He descended into the manger at Bethlehem. But the space of silence opened thus in the world is not possible without our interior silence: the silence of Bethlehem is first the one of Mary.

It is especially in our homes that this silence will first find its context: "May your house be a church," says St. John Chrysostom. And in the house there is, as in a temple, the holy of holies, the "beautiful corner," as the Russian Orthodox call it: one or more icons, a candle, a rug, and a little bench or chair. The icons of our "beautiful corner" remind us constantly of the prodigious link between personal prayer and liturgical prayer: it is the same life which is celebrated here as there. The most solitary act of the Jesus Prayer, ignored by all, is also the ecclesiastical act at its supreme sacramental level. The flame of our candle is there to remind us on what level our vigilance in daily life must be and of what fire we must burn for the world.

The Practice of the Jesus Prayer

It is, therefore, a matter of going there once or twice a day, or more according to one's opportunities. But it all depends on our decision, without which there is nothing -— no liberty, no path, no person, no sense to life. No one can take our place; once taken, it is always to be taken again, but it is only our decision which creates an existence, makes us born to ourselves, structures our depths and gives us an axis, an orientation. Through our decision everything is motivated and with it, attention, this core of the hesychast life, becomes possible. The decision seizes our whole being and indicates at every moment the status of our priorities. As long as the decision to follow Christ is not complete and total within us, renewed every day, there will be no guarantee of loyalty or non-betrayal toward the precise time which we want to consecrate regularly to our meditation. For it is there that our decision verifies itself along with the authenticity of our commitment. We have the right to be either a suicidal Judas or a Saint John who rests on the heart of Christ, but our choice must be conscious! This requirement is fundamental: on the Path, we cannot simply do here and there an exercise alongside all our other activities whenever we feel like it; the totality of the person must be involved. Prayer is not added to the rest of our life, but fertilizes the whole of it. God does not come in addition to everything else: "Who is not with Me is against Me, and he who does not gather with Me scatters" (Mt. 12:30).

All persons must find their rhythm and submit themselves to it with regularity; there is obviously no limit, for the aim of the Jesus Prayer is for it to become perpetual. Many take a half hour in the morning and another in the evening. The justification of "lack of time" does not work here: the prayer is much more nourishing and renewing than sleep. Recent research tells us that a half hour of meditation is equal to three hours of sleep. We can then without excuses or fear break through the night. And we can discover with surprise, if we take up the Jesus Prayer in all our empty moments — travel, dinner, pauses in the day and other moments in which the intellect is free —

to what extent these times add up and of what extraordinary fecundity they are! Those who do not have intellectual work are in a special position to let themselves be mobilized full-time by the prayer while their body is occupied with something else.

This watchfulness throughout the day is also a function of our sleep, for the night brings a special grace. All monks know this and, therefore, rise at night to pray. Why should lay persons deprive themselves of this? The Gospel speaks to all, and each one is called, monk or layperson, to the same height of sainthood. In the ancient Christian Tradition, there is only one spirituality without distinction; great masters like St. Nil or St. John Chrysostom estimate that all the practices of the monks should also be done by people of the world: "Rise in the middle of the night. During the night the soul is purer, lighter. Adore your Master."

Today these rhythms of humanity are no longer those of a rural society regulated by the sun and nature; prayer as asceticism in our time must occur in our depths in order to save people exhausted by technology and urbanization. If the spiritual life still rests on the same principles, these are now expressed in an existence which suffers under the weight of overwork, and it would be demonic to add yet another oppressive requirement.

The Jesus Prayer makes it possible to receive the contemporary life as an ascetic effort, transfiguring it rather than mortifying it, introducing into it a liberation necessary to incarnate grace. In this sense, prayer puts us in an attitude of interior separation in the midst of the world: an engagement and disengagement, incarnation for the purpose of deification. Each person is in this world down to the smallest detail, but never according to his or her own inclination, which is that of the prince of darkness, "murderer from the beginning, father of lies" (Jn. 8:44). It is in this darkness that our disengagement occurs, a disentanglement which is primarily active watchfulness, an alliance with the world which is always in conflict. The asceticism of prayer and attention becomes permanent, and the two blend together, for the battle is without rest: "Be watchful. Your adversary the devil prowls around like a roaring lion, seeking someone to devour" (1 Pet. 5:8).

The night symbolizes perfectly both the darkness of the world and our state of somnambulance. To break with the condition that seems normal to us "according to human perception" can introduce us into a process of radical modification of our entire being, body-soul-spirit. This is a transformation (metanoia) which opens to us the world of light. It is not a matter of imitating the monks and praying half the night, but of conquering the darkness patiently so that, in time, the Lord gives us the grace to "sleep because it is a need of nature, while my heart watches with a mad love" (St. John Climacus). The night becomes an increasingly conscious mystical state which contributes powerfully to the metamorphosis of our life.

Several important elements are to be observed in this practice:

• First, for sleep to be useful, it must be moderate: too much sleep is an injury to oneself and to God.

• Then one must learn how to fall asleep without going over the problems and worries of the day, but putting them with confidence into God's hands. This also means surrendering oneself to Him physically: relaxing the body completely, breathing deeply and slowing down little-by-little the exhalation of breath, letting it become slower and longer without any effort of the will. Once this state of complete giving over of oneself is achieved, the subconscious is opened. We can then begin to say the Jesus Prayer slowly and hear it resonate within like a lullaby, again without our will being involved. We fall asleep with the prayer filling us completely, like a sponge filling with water, into both the physical and psychic subconscious. After practicing this for a while, it sometimes happens that one can awaken in the middle of the night and hear in the depths of one's body and soul the prayer continuing by itself. Sleep then becomes transparent. The "subconscious" filled with grace does extraordinary work!

• But before coming to this stage, and in order to accompany it afterward, one must rise at night and break through this opaque darkness. Even if it is only a ray of light lasting but a few minutes, it will be enough: a hole opens in one's sleep and others will soon follow. The alarm clock can be set for three o'clock, and for a time we repeat the Jesus Prayer over and over. Returning to bed, we again relax and enter into the process of going to sleep described above. We can then, night after night, little-by-little, cover dizzying distances within our darkness and deposit there the explosive dynamism of the first Christians: "Awake, O sleeper, and arise from the dead, and Christ shall give you light" (Eph. 5:14). This is the dynamism of all spiritual life, the passage from death to Life.

• Finally, rising joyfully in the morning has always been a part of popular wisdom, but it is also a divine wisdom. A new day is given to us to live. But what sort of life? We receive it, but in order to do what? That is where it all begins, between the darkness and the light, between going to bed and rising in the morning. For whom, for what? The decision made once and for all, which creates our way of being, is renewed and focused every day and places us within our proper axis; it orients the whole day and every detail which it contains. Even if in the moment of living this experience we are unconscious of it, what counts is this profound intention to begin, there where every act takes root. The chalice of the flower is not always conscious of its roots, and yet it receives from them in every moment! The unconscious work exercised during the night will allow us to receive the day in the same state of confident surrender: "Lo, I have come to do Thy will" (Heb. 10:9; Ps. 40:9). Complete self- surrender and thanksgiving will then be the backdrop of the repetition of the Jesus Prayer from the moment we awaken. We must cling to it and not let go while doing the thousand small gestures of our toiletry, through breakfast, and during our work day and travels.

The immovable rock on which is built the foundation of our journey is the time which we dedicate exclusively to the prayer, either in the morning or in the evening or both. The place of this rendezvous of love is our "beautiful corner." Nothing in the world should keep us from this encounter, for God awaits us there and searches for us like a fiancé even before we come to it. "Come, my beloved, come! Show me your face, let me hear your voice!" (Song of Songs 2:13-14).

To turn over the prayer to one's desires of the moment means that our faith has not understood anything about the incredible reality of the relationship between God and human beings.

It is this presence which commands all our attitudes when we enter the holy place and during the prayer. We are awaited, searched for, loved by the amazing love of the One who is already there. Th is vivid consciousness engenders the "trembling before the Holy," and not one of our gestures should be done thoughtlessly. It is called ritual, like gestures of tenderness and of reciprocal rapprochement which two lovers experience when they court each other. If the ritual is often empty, it is because this phenomenal content is lacking! Yet liturgy is only that, and all our life must become this experience as well.

It all begins face to face in the secret of solitude. Our body is both the temple of this rite and the nuptial chamber of this encounter. We approach God first with our body. It alone is the strongest word that we address to our Creator, whether this carnal prayer be the cry of the world or the song of its beauty: body- tomb or prison as the Greeks called it, body of death according to St. Paul, body annihilated by suffering or by sin, carrying all the wounds of daily life, but equally body young and beautiful, sign of all that was promised to humanity and holding all its hopes.

Through the prayer, this consciousness makes us grow within the body of Christ where we decipher the full meaning of this "word" which is our body. Through Christ in whom "the whole fullness of deity dwells bodily," the body of flesh is introduced into the heart of the Divine Trinity, and our body becomes a dazzling path, a sacrament of the One who was incarnated within it. On the way, the body expresses the mystery of the person, and it lives the mysteries of Christ so that it may be born to the divine reality. God took on a body to experience humanity, and humanity by living fully its body, experiences God!

On this path, the body ceases to be a stranger. We do not have a body as an object: to the extent that we are also our body, we unite with it and experience in all fullness the word which it announces to us. We move from a body that we possess or which possesses us and others, to a body of offering and celebration, a liturgical body on the way to transfiguration, assimilated into the body of Christ.

The consciousness of our body is fi lled with this eff ort when we come into our place of meditation for such a begetting. And since our body is our way of being here in the world, it is through this way of being that we make our entrance into the prayer, which in a very realistic way puts the whole self into this exercise. Transparence comes only at this price. "Each must choose his way and that which will work best for him," wrote Theophan the Recluse. "The attention of the soul depends also on the appropriate position of the body." The hesychast Fathers gave us three ways of sitting:

(1) The posture of Elisha the Prophet (I Kgs 18:42). Th e Bible describes it in this way: "bowing toward earth, he placed his face between his knees." Saint Gregory Palamas advises this way of sitting for beginners and states that "the most perfect adopted this attitude during prayer and drew upon themselves the benevolence of God … Elisha himself, the most perfect of those who saw God, having leaned his head on his knees and having thus brought together with great effort his spirit within himself, put an end to the drought." This posture is well-known among Muslims and is currently practiced in yoga under the name of "folded leaf ": Sitting between the heels, we bend forward until the head touches the ground, the forehead pressed against the knees; the arms resting on the ground, on both sides of the legs, palms toward the sky; the body is folded in three: the thighs on the legs, the chest on the thighs.

(2) The posture of coiling up the body. Sitting on one's heels, on

a little bench or on a blanket placed on one's heels, we incline the top of the body until the chin is placed against the chest, the trunk rolling into a half circle, "in a unified form which gives the same continuity as a wheel" (Dionysius the Areopagite). "Not only will man gather himself externally conforming to an interior movement which he seeks for his spirit, but in giving such a posture to his body, he will send toward the interior of the heart the power of the spirit which flows out to the exterior." Indeed, the "spirit comes back upon itself, its movement is circular, which is its proper activity" (Gregory Palamas).

This posture is even more clearly seen in the activities of the hesychast monks who seek to subdue "the power of the beast" through the humiliation of the body. What was possible to robust men of another period, vivified by the contact with nature and overseen by a spiritual father, is not recommended for a city dweller whose backbone is already damaged by mechanized transport. Nevertheless, if he takes this way of sitting, it must be under the advice and guidance of an Elder and for brief moments only.

(3) Sitting on one's heels or on a small bench. On our knees on a blanket, the tips of the feet lightly covering one another, we sit between the heels. The knees can be together or spread out. In the beginning, a cushion or a blanket placed between the heels and the buttocks will make the sitting less painful, or sitting on a small bench that can be lowered until one can sit on one's heels.

This way of sitting is probably the most traditional one and perhaps the most agreeable for all. What is most important is sitting straight. "Be like a violin string, tuned to the right note, without too much tension or slackness," says Theophan the Recluse; "the body straight, the shoulders at ease."

The simplest way to find the proper vertical position with one's center of gravity in the stomach and not in the chest or the shoulders, is to lean forward until one's forehead touches the ground, then reconstruct the vertical position by unrolling the backbone, vertebra by vertebra. Having come to the head, stretch out the backbone a bit and let it sit on itself without collapsing toward the bottom or becoming stiff at the top. The backbone must be straight and supple. The pelvis is lightly balanced toward the front, without curving in at the ribs.

In this posture, we are like trees solidly rooted in the ground. The vertical position rests on the pelvic region which is our foundation. But rooting oneself in the ground depends entirely upon a good letting go of the top of the body which is the seat of the ego. Without sinking in on oneself, one must first relax the neck and the shoulders at the beginning of each exploration. This letting go of oneself in the shoulders is then followed automatically by a great movement of confidence toward the lower. At the end of the exploration, one is literally sitting in one's base, which, in its turn, expands, relaxes and takes root. If the exploration is gently but firmly directed toward the lower, without any effort, the lower stomach frees itself easily. In prolonging the exploration a little, the abdominal lining is gently tensed, which permits one to feel a force in the whole region of the base, but especially under the navel. The whole now acquires an immovable stability, a center of gravity, and the body can relax itself in an attitude of listening and receptivity.

The experience will show us that this way of sitting signifies much more than a way of holding oneself physically. It leads to an evolution, a profound transformation of the person. The spirit of the prayer is incarnated in matter and we become conformed to our call: the Word becomes flesh. It is an attitude of transparence to the invisible which permits God to act within us. Without rooting ourselves in our humanity, the heart does not open itself. But to find one's earthly roots is the work of the human being; opening the heart is the work of God.

The Bible is filled with examples of the necessity of an earthly rooting for the prayer to bear its fruit. One of the most extraordinary texts on this subject is the parable of the sower (Mt. 13, Mk. 4, Lk. 8), in which Jesus gives an analogy of a person in prayer and shows that very little happens in someone who has no "depths of soil" or "roots in himself" (Mk. 4, 5, and 17). Saint Paul utilizes the same realistic and carnal language in which the body is never excluded: "be rooted and grounded in love" (Eph. 3:17). This consciousness is most clearly seen in silent sitting where nothing escapes the attention, especially the tensions which offer only a rock to the prayer, leaving it on the exterior, far from the "good earth" (Mk. 4, 5, 17). In taking the navel as center of gravity, for "the law of my God is in the middle of my stomach" (Gregory Palamas), and in seeking to slow one's breathing, the Fathers of the Philokalia are not giving us recipes, but are simply honest with the movement of incarnation which transforms the innards of a human being into the womb of life. (The word "mercy" which is so often found in the Bible comes from the Hebrew *rehem*, which signifies the womb, the innards of love.)

There is something to be rediscovered by a Christianity which has fallen into intellectual abstraction, while its God took on a body. "All those who experience this can only laugh when they are rebuffed by inexperience ... those sterile propositions of petty quibblers" (Gregory Palamas). We find the same biblical ideas, now made occult, in ancient iconography, both in the east and in the west. No one can now explain to us the meaning of these Christs or saints, shown with protruding stomachs in the manner of the Buddha, or those concentric circles on the abdomen, except for people who have gone to practice *Hara* in Japan. Hara means stomach in Japanese and in the Bible: innards, roots, the depths of the earth, the foundations. Anthony Bloom states that the corporal criteria are superior to the psychological ones, because they are not subject to interpretations and errors.

(4) Other postures. For those who find it difficult to take on the

postures described, it is possible to meditate seated on a chair. To do so, do not lean back against the chair, but sit on the forward edge, legs perpendicular to the ground, feet parallel, soles firmly planted on the ground or preferably crossed at the ankles. The knees must always be lower than the pelvis, otherwise the vital center does not liberate itself and the process of taking root described above is difficult to attain. There is nothing wrong with standing up in prayer. Certain hesychast saints stood in the same spot for hours. One can imitate them as long as one maintains complete immobility, as in every posture, without rigidity in the knees, the pelvis slightly balanced toward the rear; proceed then as one would in the sitting positions.

In the standing position, the arms should loosely hang next to the body; when sitting (except in the posture of Elisha) the hands can take several positions — either placed on the legs, palms toward the sky, or falling freely between the legs, the forearms resting on the top of the thighs — or the back of one hand resting in the palm of the other, the two hands and the forearms forming a great cup, symbol of the interior cup.

In the vertical postures, the holding of one's head is very important. If it is too far forward or backward, the neck breaks the continuity of the vertical position and inhibits the descent into oneself. The quality of the circulation is very different depending on the position of the head. In order to align the neck with the backbone, the chin must be

brought in somewhat which stretches the vertebrae while keeping
contact with the ceiling or the sky. Rooted in the sky, rooted in the
earth — this is the double polarity of the human being.

Finally, the eyes remain partly closed during the prayer. One will
do this when noticing how much quicker progress is made when the
eyes are not completely closed. Falling asleep no longer happens, and
distractions of all kinds along with dreamy evasions tend to
disappear. Moreover, contact with the external world is fundamental
in a spirituality of incarnation: one does not live with one's eyes
closed!
Therefore, with eyes half-open, eyelids relaxed, we place a neutral
look on a point at a distance of a yard in front of us without seeing
anything in particular.

Whatever way of sitting is chosen, begin the time of prayer with
a profound inclination in which the Holy Spirit is invoked: "No one
can say Jesus is Lord except by the Holy Spirit" (1 Cor. 12:3). He is
our interior master, and He alone can pray within us. We are to join
ourselves to His prayer. Anyone can call upon the Holy Spirit in his
or her own way, very simply, with words of friendship and
confidence. But we can also use an invocation of the Church such as
the following:
King of Heaven, Counselor, Spirit of Truth
You who are everywhere present and fill all things,
Giver of life, come and remain within us,

Purify us of all blemish and save our souls,

You who are goodness!

This invocation is in direct continuity with the liturgy of the Church. Just as we call down the fire of the Spirit on the bread and the wine, we call it down upon ourselves as well, so that through the Jesus Prayer, He transforms us into the body and blood of Christ. As we will see later on, this prayer is profoundly eucharistic.

It is then indispensable to place on the cross of Christ all that is not well within us and around us: our worries and our problems, our burdens whatever they may be. "Come to me, all who labor and are heavy laden, and I will give you rest" (Mt. 11:28). Otherwise it is not possible to pray, because worry is our primary enemy. It can lay siege to our consciousness and render it impermeable to God. Like "thorns," worries "suffocate" the prayer which "remains barren" (Mt. 13:22).

What a paradox it is to want to pray to the infinitely merciful Father, without having confidence in Him and still clutching to one's problems! But that which obstructs our heart most is the lack of forgiveness. It is useless to begin our prayer as long as we have not forgiven from the bottom of our hearts (Mt. 18:35). Jesus is clear on this point: "If you are offering your gift at the altar, and there remember that your brother has something against you, leave your gift there before the altar and go, first be reconciled to your brother, and then come and offer your gift " (Mt. 5:23). These words are also spoken by the prophets who railed against "vain oblations." Isaiah says: "What to me is the multitude of your sacrifices? says the Lord; I have had enough of burnt offerings … my soul hates them … I will hide my eyes from you; even though you make many prayers, I will not listen; your hands are full of blood. Wash yourselves; make yourselves clean; remove the evil of your doings from before my eyes" (Is. 1:11–17). Who would still dare the blasphemy of praying in spite of that?

One must forgive all persons in our life, far and near, who have wounded us consciously or unconsciously, regardless of the greatness of the wrongdoing. We must also ask forgiveness for the wounds which we have inflicted. Before God, the best way to forgive is to ask the Lord to bless this or that person (Lk. 6:28; 1 Pet. 3:9). Before beginning the prayer, we should be able to treat any person as the one who is dearest to us on earth, and we must forgive every day until that is the case! This inner freedom is a path which never ceases to deepen.

Our hatreds are so hidden within us that it is better not to live in illusions and begin again to forgive. The prayer will then lead us into the very movement of redemption and everything will be cleansed in the blood of Christ: "*Have pity on me, a sinner!*" All this does not take very long, a few minutes at the most. One then rises from one's prostration, according to the chosen posture, and since our soul is now in peace, our body can enter into it also. We begin by relaxing our entire body: "Before praying," says Origen, "relax and rediscover the silence." A constriction somewhere in the body is always a block on the interior path: it reveals a distortion of the whole personality, a contraction of the self on its acquired positions or a will to affirm oneself against all one's fears and insecurities. As long as our body is still tense, it means that our soul is not really at peace. The smallest worry tenses us, the lack of forgiveness closes us physically. The body allows us to read our interior truth, and contributes powerfully to letting go.

The simplest way is to slowly go over one's body from the head to the feet or vice versa, feeling each part from within, remaining a while in each place and becoming conscious of the depths of the sensation, even if at this stage our consciousness is not yet enlightened by the Spirit. The body then becomes permeable to one's consciousness, "it resonates in accord with the soul" (Gregory Palamas), and these unconscious obscure parts become more and more conscious because "we place within them the law of intelligent consciousness which combats this empire" (Palamas). Once we are finished going over the body, we try to feel our whole body at once, feeling oneself from within. Each exploration deepens the relaxation of our whole being. Our whole being breathes, we are breathed in. We must feel this and become conscious of it.

That which, in the beginning, seemed to be only an exercise in relaxation will quickly lead us toward coming into the Presence, and entering the hesychast silence.

The tremendous discoveries of the Desert Fathers who, through silence of the soul and body, achieved this inviolable tranquillity of the heart," and this "sovereign liberty" (John Cassian), knew this nearly two thousand years before us. Today the work of neurophysiologists scientifically verifies their spiritual experiences: a sensation received in a pure state operates an immediate disconnection of the nervous centers and places the soul and the body in silence. We can be dissociated at any other moment, but the instant of sensation is necessarily the one of psychological presence. Human beings cannot feel and think at the same time, and this is a great secret which can become a powerful way. Moreover, attention is in direct proportion to relaxation. The more we are tense, the more we are distracted, pulled out of ourselves. "Sensation regularizes and harmonizes the function of the brain," says Dr. Vittoz. "It stimulates and regenerates the nervous cells; bit by bit it establishes a sort of silence in the brain, it is at rest … This is a recreation, a journey toward freedom."

Not to put to work the extraordinary wealth which is within us is to have contempt for the gift s God has given us. It is absurd to pray to God to ask Him for what He has already given us! "Present your bodies as a living sacrifice (Rom. 12:1) … The body is meant for the Lord, and the Lord for the body … Do you not know that your bodies are members of Christ? So glorify God in your body" (1 Cor. 6:13–19).

Before beginning the prayer, the Fathers considered one other thing very important: warming the heart. For the dissipated intellect does not enter into itself and does not unify itself to the heart unless attention is drawn to it through warming it up.

There are several ways to warm the heart. Often this happens at the moment of asking for forgiveness, when we have a broken heart (Ps. 51:17) at the sight of our sins and when we are distressed to tears over the evil we have done. We can feel this state profoundly, and that is all that is needed — the heart is wounded and our consciousness converted. "Let us warm our conscience," says John Chrysostom. "Let us afflict our soul by the memory of our sins for affliction and tribulation bring together the intellect and make it enter into itself." Let us consider that we are nothing and that if we live in this moment it is only by divine mercy.

Before entering into prayer, another helpful activity is to accompany this interior repentance with one's expressive movements. In sitting, we lean forward toward the front and rise up several times or, standing, we bow down, touching our forehead to the ground. The movement is more fluid if we bend the knees at the same time, using our hands to descend and rise.

If our heart still does not become inflamed, we will need the help of a way which has proven itself in our past and which hasprofoundly touched, seized or shaken us: an icon, an image, a work of art, the countryside, a passage from Scripture or from the Fathers, a Psalm; one can also sing a liturgical song or take up a prayer which goes straight to the heart, or a page from a spiritual book which has overwhelmed us and to which we return over and over again. The biographies of the saints are obviously an extraordinary stimulus on the way and should never leave us. We also have the prayer of our readings. In a biography, the saint presents himself to us mysteriously; we feel him or her more and more intimately, and then we speak to him, he becomes our companion on the way in a very real manner. No one can describe what such a friendship brings to us.

Among the great ways to warm our heart, there is also our unutterable experiences of the past, those privileged moments in which we have been filled with a burst of light, warmth, and happiness. We will always remember the hour, the place and the day when these seismic shakings of our whole being happened to us. These starry hours are found throughout our life from earliest infancy. Everyone knows these moments which have marked them forever. This is not a matter of "souvenirs," but of the cry of suffocating being within us. Our heart had opened itself to us in a moment and we were submerged by its content. We must renew our ties with these awesome experiences, incorporate ourselves to them, let ourselves relive their particular "quality," relish this taste, this atmosphere proper to the heart which is our ontological dimension in which we participate in the divine life.

These experiences, as numerous and varied as they may be, always reveal the same thing, and this same reality touches us in our depths here and now; it is our true being and we must open ourselves to it.

As the complete immobility of the body becomes extreme vigilance to the present moment, we begin to say the prayer out loud, letting it resonate in our ears, chewing each word with loving adoration, entirely absorbed by it: "Lord Jesus Christ, Son of God, have mercy on me, a sinner." This is done without any effort at emotion. If the heart is warmed, we pray with all our heart — the intellect and the heart united. After each invocation out loud, we let ourselves be consciously breathed in by the divine breath, being complete receptivity to this breath of life which God breathes into us. Then, breathing out, we say again: "Lord Jesus Christ, Son of God, have mercy on me, a sinner."

After a number of invocations, each person can feel from within the moment when he or she can say it to themselves, still chewing each word with lips, mouth and all that serves to create speech. We should not concern ourselves with our breathing but simply repeat one invocation after another.

One must enter into the prayer with an unshakable determination, giving no attention to any thought, good or bad. Everything is dependent upon this determination at the beginning of our prayer.

To be unfocused and start with slackness is to offer a good meal to the demon! And he will do anything to demolish our prayer. For the prayer is nothing less than a battle, and we shed blood until the death of the ego. Behind distraction is the devil (*dia-bolos* — to throw into division), and we crush him by our incessant prayer. "Strike your adversary with the name of Jesus," says John Climacus. "There is no more powerful weapon on earth or in the heavens." As soon as we give way to a thought or an image that we become interested in for however short a time and dialogue with it, all is over! We must literally close our intellect within the words of the prayer and keep it captive.

If the battle becomes too difficult, it is helpful to say the prayer again out loud and to humbly take up our prayer rope as a concrete remembrance. The devil assails us, but God allows him to do this for our greater good. Once we are placed in the hands of God, everything is grace and we are guided by Him: the main point is then to live fully what He gives us in this moment, whether it be joy, combat, or martyrdom. Thank you Lord, for all these gifts, You alone know why I must live this now! Only this attitude of patience and confidence, of perseverance in the battle, will lead us forward. And if we are distracted while our lips repeat the prayer mechanically, let us not be crushed. Saint Nicephorus gives this counsel to those who have no success:

"Repeat the prayer in the name of Jesus incessantly. In the beginning, the attention will be a stranger to it; little by little the intellect will listen to the words and the attention will fi x itself to them. Then the heart will be moved, and the prayer will enter by itself into your sanctuary." Indeed, experience shows us that a monotonous repetition appeases an intellect always in need of analysis and reflection. By imposing a single thought, the multitude of thoughts leave us, attention unifies itself and our being progressively finds its axis and orientation.

Nothing is more helpful in finding this interior attention than a completely relaxed body. We must come back to this many times on the Way: letting go of our body, surrendering ourselves. "Everything succeeds with perseverance, the Gospel makes it clear: the deserter leaves at the last moment, the one who perseveres to the end is saved!" The most important thing is to not look too much at oneself or at one's problems, but to believe in the love of God for us, even if we are distracted. Otherwise, it is selfish love which takes over.

This is called the "mechanical" phase of the prayer, the first one to be gone through, and must not be passed over. "The beginning is half of the whole," said Aristotle, and to start off wrong is never to arrive. Our mouth and our ears, which are used to so much chatter, to vain words and false foods, fill themselves with the unique word, source of all others, and learn the confession of faith for which they have been created. It is a long and difficult articulation, sometimes painful like all birthing, in which the word spells out its creation and makes all things new. There in our mouth the words lose their abstraction, we can feel them physically with our lips, tongue, larynx and relish them. Their vibration on our vocal cords adjust our whole being to them, aligning it to its true tonality, and their resonance in our ears make us conceive the word through listening. For Mary, all began with listening, said St. Augustine, and submitting herself entirely to the word through obedience, she received in her body that which she first heard through her ears: "Let it be to me according to your word … And the word became flesh" (Lk. 1:38; Jn. 1:14).

The right action of an expressed word is to incorporate itself into the one who listens and submits himself to it. The revolutionary work of Father Marcel Jousse showed us scientifically that human beings are by nature "imitators" who repeat to our body in interior micro-gestures the words which are heard. The vibration penetrates the body and models it through miming, impacting our entire psychosomatic nature. We hear a word and eat it.

This phenomenon, which Jousse calls *intussusception* (from the Latin, intus — interior, and suscipere — to receive), is well known in the teachings of traditional societies, particularly among the Hebrews and the Palestinians in the time of Jesus. This is how they learned the Torah by heart and how Jesus Himself taught.

This principle of the word which "echoes itself" has become the basis of our liturgy. It should also be in our catechesis (from the Greek catecho, which means to repeat as an echo!) and in all of prayer. The word is eaten, and that which we eat vivifies and transforms us, because we have assimilated it, and we then become what we eat and we can only witness to that which we ourselves have become. "Son of man, eat what is offered to you; eat this scroll, and go, speak to the house of Israel ... Son of man, eat this scroll that I give you and fill your stomach with it" (Ezek. 3:1–3).

The Jesus Prayer summarizes the whole Bible in a unique expression born from the experience of our fathers. The word follows the same path as our consciousness and enters into its depths where it incarnates itself through a progressive infusion.

This eating of the prayer, alternatively out loud and silently, can last a long time. It is not up to us to decide the length of this stage. The work done here is of such importance that it would be wrong to cut it short. But one day we will discover, through grace and our perseverance, that the prayer ceases to be mechanical and has gone beyond our lips: we are in the second phase called "mental"; it is then expressed in our mind where it has made inroads, received by a mold which the previous stage has prepared. The monks often stayed many years in the vocal phase, seeking humbly to join to their prayer the fulfillment of the commandments of Christ in their daily life. In this conversion, there is no progress without the prayer, and only the fire of repentance opens the door from one stage to another.

In the "mental" phase, even if the corporal mechanism does not function on the exterior, the prayer is always "corporal" and will be experienced physically more and more. In the intellect, the words articulate themselves consciously, resonate to our interior ears and can be visualized, especially as an exercise of penetration at the beginning of this stage. We can, for example, with eyes closed, trace in large writing one word of the prayer after the other in a slow rhythm. We can write "Lord" feeling the movement of the hand and the arm writing one letter after the other, then see the word in its entirety, looking at it without thinking and letting it enter into ourselves, in the body, identifying ourselves with it through a kind of direct contact between oneself and the word, seeing first in the intellect and then in the chest.

Taking one's time, we do the same with the other words: "Jesus" — "Christ" — and at the end seeing the whole sentence in this way. "An image visualized in the organism has a profound effect on the one who works at it," said Dr. Lefebure in his book *Rhythmic Breathing*. Once again, science only confirms the old experiences of our tradition. This effect is well-known through the contemplation of icons and "Christ Himself, for this reason, taught through images and parables: the image acts profoundly on the human soul, on its creative faculties," adds St. John of Kronstadt (1829–1908). "We say, for example, that if in the time which precedes the birth of a child, a mother frequently looks upon the face or the portrait of her beloved spouse, the child will resemble the father much more; or if she looks frequently at the portrait of a pretty child, she will give birth to a beautiful baby. If the Christian often looks with love and piety upon the image of our Lord Jesus Christ, of His very pure Mother and of the saints, his soul will receive the spiritual traits of the face lovingly contemplated: gentleness, humility, mercy, temperance. If we contemplate more often the images and especially the life of our Lord and of the saints, how much we will change, how we will journey from height to height!"

The word seen, heard, and felt from within is no longer the same. Often, it surrounds itself with light and makes joy and peace rise within when we unite with it; just like the icon, where this process is undoubtedly easier for it is made for plunging into the one who looks at it and filling him or her with its uncreated light. But with the icon, there is no need to make an effort; the icon is an integral part of the life of the Christian who lives in its familiarity.

These preliminary exercises are not indispensable, any more than the following, but to the extent that they express the consciousness of our misery and the humility of our search for God, then they are truly an asceticism of transfiguration and can become true prayer. In this "mental" phase of the Jesus Prayer, we remain sitting silently, the intellect alone repeating the invocations with loving adoration as before. Consciousness, here, can be so absorbed by the prayer that it identifies itself to it; at this moment, the soul is freed from its enemies — multiple thoughts.

4. St. John of Kronstadt, *My Life in Christ*

But the more the prayer interiorizes itself, the more we become sensitive to what is most interior within us: breath. As though the prayer had come to name its presence, we open ourselves to its mystery: Is not the breath the true revealer of the name? Our breathing being perpetual, the Creator has deposited in our own intimacy the most extraordinary way to encounter Him. From the beginning, we have been conscious of this and it was taken for granted by the ancients:

"May the remembrance of Jesus be one with your breathing, and then you will know the usefulness of the hesychia," said St. John Climacus in the seventh century; he recommended that we "glue" the name of Jesus to our breathing. A little later, the unknown authors of the Centuries took up this text and emphasized that "the Jesus Prayer must be breathed continually."

Did not the psalmist pray: "With open mouth I pant, because I long for Thy commandments"? (Ps. 119:131) The entire Bible opens itself through this foundational verse: "Then the Lord God formed man of dust from the ground, and breathed into his nostrils the breath of life; and man became a living being" (Gen. 2:7). This is the creative act par excellence which the resurrected Christ will reiterate at the new creation: "He breathed on them" (Jn. 20:22), a gesture which the priest remembers in breathing on each baptized person born to the true life.

Breathing is the great movement of life, not only of its birth but of its continual metamorphosis within us. We must become conscious of this in the prayer, which brings together the word and the breath, making of our way of breathing a path of transparence to mystery. Interior listening and consciousness of the breath leads little by little to calmness in the body and the soul, to a disconnection of the ego and all its tensions. We may experience, at the end of exhalation, that mysterious moment of deep silence which is both strange and familiar. This brief instant expands as we surrender ourselves to it. It will progressively reveal itself as a presence: it is Someone. And this silence becomes the source of life in our depths when it breathes into us our inhaling. It expresses itself in us, structures and gives us form; it is the word which becomes flesh within us. At the end of inhaling, there is a new silence; from there will come the exhalation which makes the vivifying breath, the creative energy, the pneuma- Spirit penetrate right into our cells and the marrow of our bones.

Each inhalation is, therefore, the receiver of the divine breath, a rising toward the light which enlightens our consciousness through this mystery; each expiration is a descent toward the depths to receive this unknown being who nevertheless resembles us.

The tradition proposes several possibilities for the prayer: aft er our preparation and going over the body which will have opened us and relaxed us, we must become conscious of the breath as described above. Our whole being breathes and feels it in depth for several moments. In no case should we "make" the breathing voluntary, but let it make itself. Inhalation which comes from the depths of the abdomen is a visitation: God breathes into us His breath and we inhale it; we must receive it consciously and at each exhalation surrender ourselves consciously to it, relax ourselves in Him.

As we come to rest (hesychia), exhalation slows and becomes deeper: "Retain your breath a bit, do not breathe too boldly," said Gregory the Sinaite. Then we say the prayer simply on this rhythm: "Lord Jesus Christ" breathing in "Son of God" during the silence at the end of the inhalation "Have mercy on me, a sinner" while breathing out. This is the most classic form of the prayer. If this proves to be too difficult, we can adopt the following approach. Dividing the prayer into four, we say:

"*Lord Jesus Christ*" breathing in

"*Son of God*" breathing out

"*Have pity*" breathing in again

"*on me, a sinner*" breathing out

Some very tense people cannot let any word come in on the inhalation and can only say it while exhaling, dividing it according to the length of their exhalation, sometimes saying only one word at a time.

One can also say the prayer all at once according to one of the ways mentioned, then be silent for several breaths, letting it resonate within. From all eternity, silence rests in the name and it is silence which reveals it through the power of the Spirit-breath. "The Word comes out of an abyss of silence, pronounces a brief word, and returns into this abyss of silence," says an adage of the Fathers. But when silence itself seizes us, the words of the prayer disappear entirely, and the Spirit of fire makes of us a living torch, for the name of the word is light. In that burning we are silent.

This rhythm of breathing "was given to us by the Creator to allow divine life to take hold of the depths of our being and fill our entire existence with light."

The rhythm of breath is so intimately linked to the heart and blood, that the Jesus Prayer will one day be able to descend into the heart and into the pulsations of the blood which spread throughout the whole body. This is the work of grace, in which the prayer becomes spontaneous; it says itself in our depths, running on its own without voluntary effort on our part. This is the third stage which is called "contemplative."

The heart, and with it our whole being, is set on fire by grace which now takes complete charge of the prayer, often inundating us with joy and love, and sometimes with the vision of the Taboric light. Here the name offers its powerful energy in the measure in which we can support it. It is a fire which devours passions, according to Hebrews 12:29. Chasing the demons out of our heart, we begin an unmatched combat against these powers to which are joined the "spiritual hosts of wickedness in the heavenly places" (Eph. 6:12). As

Father Sophrony says: "The number of trials through which passes the asceticism of this prayer is indescribable ….. we must have either great experience or a teacher … and everyone must have a prudent watchfulness, the spirit of contrition, the fear of God and the patience to bear all that can happen to us; then only will it become a force which unites our spirit with the Spirit of God and will little by little, after many years, become an integral part of our being, and our nature itself will be spiritualized, even in our reflexes."

Every true prayer, said in humility, leading to the death of self and surrender into the hands of God, ends in this inflaming of the heart which can never be the result of our efforts and exercises. Voluntary cupidity might easily, through artificial means, fix a false attention to the heart, while the prayer may not be there since it is a gift from God! From such deceit we could expect all sorts of manifestations of passions, of cardiac or nervous disorders, of mental imbalance, but especially of never again having access to depths of the heart, the "locus Dei" guarded by the flaming cherubim whose door no one can ever force open.

What needs to be said about certain texts of the Philokalia, and even of The Way of the Pilgrim, is that they are very dangerous for amateurs who abuse them. These methods which "force the intellect to descend into the heart," to "close" it by "pushing" within with the breath and to bring the prayer in rhythm with its beating, were put into writing for monks who were personally overseen by an Elder, day after day, step by step, situated in the context of an ecclesial, sacramental and ascetic life. We are not to prohibit these methods: they are transmitted to us by saints, but we ought to approach them as they did, accompanied by an experienced guide, within the Church, and not as an apprentice sorcerer. This must be clear: "Every Christian can attain the heights of the Jesus Prayer without any other technique than that of charity and obedience. Here interior disposition is everything. The Jesus Prayer is sufficient unto itself, it makes us free of everything except Jesus."

What is risked when we approach the door of heaven in our depths without being accompanied by an "angel," who has already come along that path, is not a risk when it comes to the body and to our breathing as we have described them. The methods are dangerous if they are reduced to a formula which is forced to produce grace; this would be an attempt to violate God and to have power over Him.

In taking a body to encounter us, God reveals interior continuity, a fundamental connection between human nature and grace. Th ere is no "natural" on one side and "supernatural" on the other, but a true correspondence, a reciprocal participation and communion between the human and the divine. With the incarnation of Christ, the human body has come to its earthly fulfillment, created according to a Christocentric structure and, therefore, ontologically capable of extending the incarnation within it. Thus, "God is present to all things," says Dionysius the Aeropagite, "but all things are not present in Him."

The prayer of the "heart," and therefore of the "body," makes us become conscious of this presence and of our original divine relationship in which the body makes itself the path of the "transmutation of the senses" of which Gregory Palamas speaks, until "it attains the fullness of Christ" (Eph. 4:13). This is truly the profound characteristic of Christian asceticism, its inner meaning, and that which distinguishes it from all other asceticism or exercise. This is where it stops being ideology and abstract Platonism.

If we are conscious of this reality, everything is found in the secret orientation of our desire which makes a prayer of the most intimate gesture, an action inhabited by grace. Outside of this fundamental perspective, we fall precisely into a "recipe" or a kind of mind-body culture for the liberation of self by self. "Sin is crouching at the door" (Gen. 4:7), and we are never safe from falling into it, from wanting to engender ourselves through ourselves, and to find again in some unconscious corner that old ambition of humanity: doing without God. Our efforts are then completely ineffective; we can do nothing by ourselves, other than give birth to a monster of pride. "There is a way which seems right to a man, but its end is the way to death" (Prov. 16:25). What guide is more blind than our own self? Only the Church, treasure house of wisdom, can keep us from the wrong path.

Chapter Four

THE JESUS PRAYER
AS A WAY OF LIFE

Follow me.

Mark 2:14

The Jesus Prayer is first of all a confession of faith which contains the faith of all our ancestors and engenders us into the constant memory of all the marvels that God realized through them. Th e biblical revelation is revelation for us today. In opening the Bible, we discover the ways of God toward us which the name of Jesus carries to their supreme realization.

The Jesus Prayer must then be nourished and impregnated by a great familiarity with the Bible. The name is the word which contains all words. Through this slow and loving impregnation, the Bible makes its spirit penetrate us and, through the prayer, it transforms our deepest attitudes. The true content of the Jesus Prayer is the Bible, and the Bible finds in the prayer one of its primary ways of developing our fundamental attitudes. Through the Jesus Prayer, we learn to live from the words instead of only reading them. We simply learn to live, to let go of our fears and of our ego, entering into the "covenant of fire" with the One who will lead us into a different way of being.

Jehoshaphat, King of Judea, surrounded by the Moabites and facing certain annihilation, cried toward God: "We are powerless against this great multitude that is coming against us. We do not know what to do, but our eyes are upon Thee." God answered: "Fear not, and be not dismayed at this great multitude; for the battle is not yours but God's" (2 Chron. 20:12 and 15). What an extraordinary revelation! It is not for us to manage our life, we are not masters of history for God alone is the Master. This battle of life is not ours, but His. "You will not need to fight in this battle; take your position, stand still, and see the victory of the Lord on our behalf" (v. 17). This is a stunning promise, if Jehoshaphat adopts the "right position." And which one is that? Putting oneself entirely in God's hands, in complete confidence, so as not to keep Him from acting. At the very moment when all appearances point to the contrary, at the height of panic before certain death which this immense army of enemies was about to inflict on them, "Jehoshaphat bowed his head with his face to the ground, and all Judah and the inhabitants of Jerusalem fell down before the Lord, worshipping the Lord" (v. 18).

The Jesus Prayer repeated tirelessly before an event presenting itself to us allows us to "bow" before God who acts in the event. And because He acts, we are to worship Him, to surrender ourselves to Him in the certainty of our faith. At the beginning of the battle, Jehoshaphat cried: "Hear me, Judah and inhabitants of Jerusalem! Believe in the Lord your God, and you will be established; believe His prophets, and you will succeed" (v. 20). Then they moved forward saying, "Give thanks to the Lord, for His steadfast love endures forever," and at that moment "the Lord set an ambush" against the enemy (v. 22).

The Bible gives us here an extreme example in which our logic is thrown aside, but this is always the case, for "your ways are not My ways" (Is. 55:8). Our taking up the right position is perhaps even more difficult in the banality of the daily grind rather than in exceptional situations. The prayer, then, "holds us together," as the text says, in a proper position according to our faith which, beyond and even against all reason, allows us to "bow"; that is, to submit ourselves to the acting love of God, to believe and to adore. It is through faith that we are saved and that the impossible is accomplished.

On this subject, the Bible is of dazzling clarity and multiplies throughout its history many such scenes: after Jehoshaphat, one should read the epic of Joshua, David and Goliath, Gideon, Job. The entire biblical fabric is expressed there; it is the central theme of the Bible, the context of all the texts whether stated or not. Jesus is the fulfillment of this faith, the personifi ed incarnation of this attitude. We understand nothing of the Gospel if we do not see behind every

101

action of Christ the action of the Father whose will He accomplishes. Jesus expresses it many times: before the tomb of Lazarus, during the multiplication of the bread or at Gethsemane. He invites us to do the same: "Without Me you can do nothing" (Jn. 15).

Unfortunately, we often have a false idea of faith. We have faith when we feel something. Yet faith does not come from psychological or emotional feeling but from our decision. We can decide to believe and to have confidence — this is an act of our freedom. We are free to accept the word of God as the supreme reality for us, without considering what our emotions, our sensations and reflections tell us in their tyranny. The great promises contained in the Bible become a fait accompli when we decide to accept them by faith! Whether we feel something or not does not enter into the picture. The one who abandons himself in faith into the hands of God — with the attitude "have mercy on me, a sinner" — is born anew through the Holy Spirit.

On the contrary, the reason for our doubts is always the same: "I do not feel anything." Then we are not only victims of our mental feelings, but we have more faith in our ego than in the word of God! The prayer comes to turn this relationship around: through it our faith is founded on what God has said and not on what we feel. "Lord I want to believe and I decide to take Your word, Your promises to the letter!" To let the prayer inhabit us through this decision takes us away little by little from the dependence and slavery of the ego which constantly manipulates us. "The truth will set you free," said Jesus (Jn. 8:32).

One must take the word of God as the truth and build upon it, then we are free. Peace and profound joy are born at that moment within us, whether our feelings are dry and empty or in turmoil. To live by faith changes everything, and that is the apprenticeship made by the one who prays. "He who believes in Me," as Scripture has said, "Out of his heart shall flow rivers of living water" (Jn. 7:38).

Through the prayer, Christ pulls us out of our subjective hell to introduce us into God who has a loving design on all humanity and on each one of us in particular. All the scriptures say it and repeat it: He has chosen you since before your birth; He knows each fi ber of your being; the least of your thoughts is familiar to Him even before it is expressed; nothing that concerns you is left to chance (Ps. 139); He seeks you constantly and never ceases to await you like a fiancé (Song of Songs, Hosea, parable of the lost sheep: Jn. 10); not a single hair falls from your head without His permission (Mt. 10:30). Finally, He dies of love for you personally and rises again to offer you fullness of life. All of that occurs here and now, within the midst of what you are living and which in the eyes of your ego is perhaps displeasing, revolting or horrible. The Apostle James said: "Count it all joy, my brethren, when you meet various trials, for you know that the testing of your faith produces steadfastness. And let steadfastness have its full effect, that you may be perfect and complete, lacking in nothing" (Jas. 1:2–4). But this assumes, as St. Paul says, that we do not let ourselves be conformed to this world, but that we offer ourselves to God as a living sacrifice.

"To offer ourselves as a living sacrifice to God" is one of the most wonderful definitions of perpetual prayer. It means to adhere fully, and with love, to that which IS, communing with the present moment as it presents itself, saying "yes" to the event which comes upon us whatever it may be, without allowing our ego to judge it, refusing to say that it is "terrible, unacceptable, horrible." All mental interpretation of an event prevents us from having the experience of providence, because every event, without exception, is its manifestation! (Is. 45:6–7; Deut. 32:39; 1 Kgs. 2:6–7; Amos 3:6; Eccl. 11:14; Job 1:21; Gen. 45:5–8; Jn. 18:11). Saint Augustine summarizes well the unanimity of the Fathers on this subject: "All that happens to us here below against our will only happens to us through the will of God, through the dispositions of providence. And if, considering the weakness of our spirit, we cannot find a reason for such-and-such an event, let us attribute it to divine providence, giving it this honor by receiving it from its hand, believing firmly that it does not send it to us without motive" (De Genesis).

That is why Christ insists so oft en: "Do not judge!" Judgment, interpretation, so many opinions in regard to everything ("what terrible weather!") puts a distance between us and the event. Our ego becomes conscious of itself by its opinions, feels itself live, infl ates itself and separates itself from the reality observed. That is exactly the definition of sin: distance, remoteness, separation, which make us lose the meaning of all that happens to us.

One of the first effects of the Jesus Prayer is to stop this attitude in us and to help us recognize the divine presence in the event by placing the holy name upon it. It is through this "method" that Christ frees us from our sins. He offers Himself completely to the will of God which He recognizes in the worst darkness of His suffering. Nothing could have been more unbearable and more horrible than the Passion of Christ. It is so utterly contrary to what He is, the God-Man, that He sweats blood over it.

There precisely, when nothing is working right in the eyes of humanity, He demonstrates before the world and to history the only possible path in the face of suffering, the only possible response to the question of suffering which humanity has never been able to answer: the acceptance of the unacceptable because the will of God expresses itself there. This is faith in its purest state since nothing keeps it from believing! And this total surrendering, in which nothing remains of our own will, allows God to act with power, to make of suffering, and even of death, a veritable alchemy. As the caterpillar enclosed in its cocoon becomes a butterfly, so we are transformed into the fullness of resurrected humanity.

This is a fundamental attitude of the disciple of Christ. Peter, James and John, the three great initiated ones, were the first to receive it in the intimacy of Christ at Gethsemane. It is the attitude of the child held in the hands of the mother, not only in suffering, but at each moment, since each moment is a trial and comes to verify our faith. Whether it be bad weather, the thousand vexations of daily life, illness or death, only a "yes" — complete and without reservation — to each event, each situation and at each moment, takes us out of sin, out of separation from God. We are one with the event, as the child is one with his mother, surrendered in her arms. Nailed on the cross, Christ is the child par excellence. "Father, into Your hands I commit My spirit," and He adds, since the secret of right attitude is now given to His disciples: "It is finished!"

Only this total acceptance, this total surrender, this "yes" without reservation to all that happens, in the conviction that God is acting and never ceases to create, makes Christ victorious over suff ering and death instead of being a victim of them. Following His example, our prayer can become at times a similar drama.

This is the "Wedding of the Lamb" from Revelation, the biblical covenant carried to its climax. As St. Paul says with power and precision: "For the Son of God, Jesus Christ, whom we preached among you, was not Yes and No; but in Him it is always Yes. For all the promises of God find their Yes in Him. That is why we utter the Amen through Him, to the glory of God" (2 Cor. 1:19).

Because God entered into history, descending right into the darkness of our human experience, and especially into our suff ering, death and all our hellish situations, the commonplace fabric of our daily life is the location of our encounter with Him, the place of the covenant, there precisely where the exchange of wills between God and persons happens. Following Christ who is only "Yes," we pronounce our "yes" by surrendering ourselves to the event, letting ourselves be crucified on the situation that is off ered: "May Thy will be done!" Then from the event, however revolting it may be to the ego, springs forth "the glory of God" as St. Paul says, and we become in turn, like Christ, the "sacrificial Lamb" and celebrate at each moment the wedding of the Lamb instead of losing ourselves in the darkness of the world.

This is where we find the secret of what is called the spiritual life and no place else. This is the kernel where the mystical life begins: it is always in the present moment that we offer our will to something. It is here and now that we make a covenant with something, that we give our heart, that we prostitute ourselves or that we are deified. The present moment is neither time nor eternity, but the point in which the two meet, and it is only on this cross, our own, that we exercise our freedom. To whom, to what do we give ourselves and surrender ourselves? We must become aware that at each moment there is a choice, that it is tragic not to live consciously, to let oneself be tossed about by events like a bottle in the ocean with no orientation. For Revelation says: "Because you are lukewarm, neither cold nor hot,

I will spew you out of My mouth" (Rev. 3:15).

The same extraordinary text continues: "Therefore I counsel you to buy from Me salve to anoint your eyes, that you may see" (v. 18). John later adds: "He who has an ear, let him hear what the Spirit is saying" (v. 22). And what does it say? How do we decipher its word behind an event brought by the present moment? "Those whom I love, I reprove and chasten" (v. 19). Here Revelation takes up the great theme of the way God teaches His children, which is found throughout the Bible. From the book of Proverbs, where we read: "For the Lord reproves him whom He loves, as a father the son in whom he delights" (Prov. 3:12) through to the epistle to the Hebrews, where we find the famous passage: "It is for discipline that you have to endure. God is treating you as sons; for what son is there whom his father does not discipline? If you are left without discipline, in which all have participated, then you are illegitimate children and not sons ... Shall we not be subject to the Father of spirits, and live? ... He disciplines us for our good, that we may share His holiness" (Heb. 12:7–13).

Here we find what we are to see in the event, but what is it that we must hear? "Behold, I stand at the door and knock; if anyone hears My voice and opens the door, I will come in to him and eat with him, and he with Me" (Rev. 3:20). In other words, the present moment is Christ Himself, for He is eternity in person entered into time; time is filled with His presence, and to unite to the moment, to commune with what is happening here and now is to enter into the intimacy of Christ, to sit at the table with Him.

This is the only way to avoid being overcome by trials, which is the final demand of our Father. On the contrary, to be victorious with Christ over suffering and death which passing time, "the devourer of peoples," contains. To vanquish time and what it contains is to transcend it by an attitude of surrender through the confident "yes" of the bride who sees in each moment a gift from the groom.

This attitude is diametrically opposed to the passivity of resignation, and especially to defeat; it engenders an action in which the supernatural forces within us are liberated; in which we center ourselves on the creative power of God and not on revolutions which only leave behind monuments to the dead.

The saints have always known how to focus their entire being on this one point. This victory is promised to each one of us in the book of Revelation: "He who conquers, I will grant him to sit with Me on My throne, as I Myself conquered and sat down with My Father on His throne" (Rev. 3:21). And this text is preceded by the words: "So be zealous and repent!" (v. 19).

It is sin which separates and distances us from God who is more objective in our life than anything which surrounds us. Th rough sin we are deaf and blind: "who have eyes to see, but see not, who have ears to hear, but hear not!" (Ezek. 12:2/Mt. 13). We are closed beings. "Behold, I stand at the door knocking" (Rev. 3:21). We must always open, for it is always God who knocks. The mind sees sometimes the good, sometimes the bad, but the vision of truth sees only the good: "All things turn to good for those who love God," said St. Paul, and that is why he can then say, "with all our affliction, I am overjoyed" (2 Cor. 7:4). For if the Christian lives, "it is no longer I who live, but Christ who lives in me" (Gal. 2:20). The suffering of the Christian is carrying the death of Christ, and when the Christian accepts this, he is conformed to Christ (Phil. 3:10).

We are "always carrying in the body the death of Jesus, so that the life of Jesus may also be manifested in our bodies" (2 Cor. 4:10). Thus understood and lived, suffering, and all that "displeases" us, is "granted to us" (Phil. 1:29) so that "an eternal weight of glory beyond all comparison" (2 Cor. 4:17) will be born within us as of now.

The marvelous proof of this statement resides in the attitude of the Apostles who, despite being whipped, insulted, and tortured, were filled with joy when they suffered for the name (Acts 5:41). We are their inheritors, disciples of Christ as they were, and all that we live can only be in His name and because of Him. When at times our existence flagellates us and we are put to trial, Jesus declares us "blessed" in the last beatitude: "Blessed are you when men revile you and persecute you and utter all kinds of evil against you falsely on My account. Rejoice and be glad ..." (Mt. 5:11, 12). Christ reveals to us that we can accept suffering because it makes us similar to Him, and then He frees us within! God has a perfect plan for history, and our work is to unite with it. The Jesus Prayer offers us this constant communion.

We are here in the presence of a radically new approach to our daily life: it is a revolutionary way of being at the heart of the agony of existence, a complete conversion of our attitudes that make us so aggressive against all that does not suit us. The true disciple of Christ is "rooted in love" (Eph. 3:17), in other words, like roots and foundations, he or she lives beyond appearances and the surface of things, conscious of the great love of God that is constantly offered to us. The disciple plunges into the depths of an event to seek an encounter with the loved One as thirsting roots plunge into the earth to find life-giving water. Each moment is, therefore, the best opportunity, and we must let none escape in order to progress on the way.

We will never hear of a saint who turns away from a trial or complains of an illness. The least vexation is a benediction for him. He rejoices in everything "in all times and in all places." Saint Paul sets the tone for this great cloud of witnesses down through history: "Rejoice in the Lord always; again I will say, Rejoice. The Lord is at hand. Have no anxiety about anything" (Phil. 4:4).

When St. Thérèse of Lisieux would see one of her novices merely frown, she scolded her immediately! The least tension in our body signifies that we rely more on ourselves than on God. For God is found in the detail, not in our well-crafted abstractions or vague generalizations which have no reality. To be attentive, fully conscious of detail, to rejoice in the minute we are living, appreciating each situation — that is the essence of the way. As little Thérèse said, "To transform everything into love from moment to moment" and to remember "that at each moment I have within my hands the incredible power to translate or betray Love." She believed, as did so many other saints, in love, no more no less, in love as source of all life, as a way to perfection, as a unique end.

It can be said that all the saints — this is the characteristic of the true disciple — have passionately deciphered in daily life the face of love inclined upon them, the face of their Master, and have given themselves to Him. It is the only attitude which lets us attain the depths of things in every moment. Then no event, however deceiving or revolting it may seem, will be an obstacle to love, and all that happens will be seen as coming from love, given to us as a way to go to Him.

To believe this is to have an experience of faith in its purest state. We lean only on what we know. Truth alone suffices and the conviction that the love of God will never pass away: "Who shall separate us from the love of Christ? Shall tribulation, or distress, or persecution, or famine, or nakedness, or peril or sword? As it is written, 'For Thy sake we are being killed all the day long; we are regarded as sheep to be slaughtered.' No, in all things we are more than conquerors through Him who loved us. For I am sure that neither death, nor life, nor angels, nor principalities, nor things present, nor things to come, nor powers, nor height, nor depth, nor anything else in all creation, will be able to separate us from the love of God in Christ Jesus our Lord" (Rom. 8:35).

From then on, there is only one effort in our life, one unique effort through all that we do from morning till night: riveting our attention on God who seeks us and loves us. To be dominated by this effort, to be literally possessed by it, is the secret of all the saints and geniuses. They bring together their energies into a single point and pursue tirelessly a great design which unites their entire existence.

For the one who constructs his life in this manner, oriented in such a radical way, everything really begins and then things go quickly, for the path is fast! In a person thus given over, completely surrendered, God never ceases to act. Even if he does not always think about it, the reins of his life are in the hands of the Lord, and it is He alone who has the initiative. This is true humility. And it is the foundation of sainthood.

The Jesus Prayer is the instrument of this breakthrough. Nothing mortifies the impulse of our nature toward independence and places us more under the hold of grace. The prayer leads us to practice the most absolute interior renunciation, attacking the ego, not in its manifestations, but at its core.

Little by little, we take on the habit of turning away from ourselves and turning toward Christ. Putting oneself in the presence of His person, which is done continually, truly modifies us. The person of Christ rubs off on us. By constantly looking at Him, He passes into us. His manner, His reactions, His thoughts become ours by a kind of contagion, by a true osmosis. This "selective miming" which psychology now values, is one of the great builders of the personality: there is nothing more formative than to be under the direct influence of a person in whom we have placed our love. But when it comes to Christ, this phenomenon is not merely a human symbiosis. It is an ontological mutation in which the "uncreated energies," that is, the very life of God, circulates within us and renders us "always more conformed to Christ" (Rom. 8:29), and progressively brings us to a resemblance of Him.

Miming, taken up by psychologists today in the service of the soul, is a mystical reality from earliest Christianity in the service of human beings for our total transformation, body- soul- spirit. When St. Paul says that he is an "imitator of Christ," he is using the secular language of the theater: the mime puts himself so completely under the skin of the character, that he takes on his traits, being so "united with Christ" (Rom. 6:5), that he makes Him visible to other people.

"It is no longer I who live, but Christ who lives in me" (Gal. 2:20). A person is unified when all the elements which constitute his life are one; that is, proceed from the same source and tend toward the same goal: Christ, to be Him, at each moment, through our gestures, words, gaze, behavior, desires ... and little by little even in our spontaneous reflexes. That is fundamental asceticism! "I have been crucified with Christ" (Gal. 2:20), according to the strong expression of St. Paul, means that it is no longer the ego which is the principle of our actions, but Christ who lives in us. Jesus Himself said on the eve of His death: "He who abides in Me, and I in him, he it is that bears much fruit, for apart from Me you can do nothing" (Jn. 15:5).

In this context, love reveals its overwhelming identity. We have made of love morality, philanthropy or devotion — even among Christians — when it reveals itself here as nothing less than the very intimacy of the life of God! It is, therefore, a matter of making the very substance of our action, the way in which we live it, becomes the life of Christ, a "demonstration of His power," as St. Paul said (1 Cor. 2:4). "In this will all men know that you are my disciples, if you have love for one another," said Jesus (Jn. 13:35). "He who loves is born of God and knows God" (1 Jn. 4:7) in the biblical sense of the word (that is, to experience). St. John continues with this insight which once again expresses the entire revelation: "In this the love of God was made manifest among us, that God sent His only Son into the world, so that we might live through Him" (1 Jn. 4:9). To love means "to live through Christ" and that is why He came among us, and then within us!

This incredible unity between persons and God, because one has surrendered entirely to the other, leads to a fusion, without confusion, as iron in fire. "The Spirit makes Christ penetrate within us to the end of our fingers; He penetrates our body," cried out St. Symeon. The whole hesychast tradition recognized it, and today

science begins to confirm it. Incorporation into Christ, which is the goal of the Jesus Prayer, changes the very substance of things, right to the marrow of our bones, even to the modification of our cellular structure.

Christianity introduces for the first time in the history of humanity a radically different vision of the body. In non-Christian religious consciousness, the body has been more or less rejected in the name of the spirit. Much of the ancient world developed an extraordinary dualism in anthropology, considering the body to be the prison of the soul. But all metaphysical understanding of the incarnation of God, which is the foundational mystery of Christianity, relies above all on the recognition of the metaphysical nature of corporality, which is expressed with great power in the teaching of the resurrection of bodies. The body is metaphysically part of our being, and death, which destroys the body, cannot completely annihilate it. "Do you not know that your body is a temple of the Holy Spirit within you, which you have from God?" said St. Paul, and "your bodies are members of Christ" (1 Cor. 6:19, 15).

116

One of the great signs of the verification of these teachings is the yearning which lives in each person from their youth, the spiritual emptiness which is felt in the body as well as in the soul. In other words, the body is not an object that we have, but the physical manifestation of the metaphysical. The physical then becomes the visible expression of the invisible mystery of being, the exteriorization on the historical plane of our interior dimension beyond space and time. To paraphrase the word "body," one would have to say that it is our "way of being here in the world." In the Old Testament, there is not even a word to designate "the body" as a reality separate from the rest! We are an inseparable whole: always in all our aspects we are spiritual and corporal (a reciprocal and total co-penetration). The juxtaposition of a body plus a soul plus a spirit is the result of the original division and of our sin which separates us. According to the greatest among the Fathers (Irenaeus, Gregory of Nyssa, Macarius, Gregory Palamas), it is the whole person who is created in the image of God. We human beings are integrally body-soul- spirit, in communion with God, and as such are "clothed with the Word and the Holy Spirit." The body itself is, therefore, made in the image of God, in the image of the body of the Word which is God incarnate. As St. Sophronius of Jerusalem (sixth century) stated: "The flesh was at the same time fl esh and fl esh of the Word of God … for it is in Him, and not in itself, that it has life." The person of Christ has penetrated our human flesh and glorified it forever by introducing the human body into the heart of the divine Trinity on the day of the Ascension.

If then it is "in Him that the body has life," it is in Him that is found its internal principle which is a spiritual one. The body is the expression of the person. In the Bible, as well as in the tradition, Manichean or Gnostic dualism, which sees evil in the body and opposes it to spirit, is ignored. And that is why Christianity has always been suspicious of both the excesses of the flesh and the excesses of asceticism. If it is true that our body is part of the spiritual path, to annihilate it or go out of it is to reject the person, the whole of our being. There is an asceticism of mortification, which treats the body like an object, and an asceticism of transfiguration which consists in harmonizing the body with the spirit. It is true that this balance is diffi cult to find, and that the saints have often gone through a stage of their lives in which they practiced terrible mortifications, but they did not mistake that as the ultimate purpose of their asceticism. "For no man ever hates his own flesh" (Eph. 5:29).

The body is a " temple," but not in the manner of a house which shelters a tenant, for this would still be duality. The body is inhabited by the Holy Spirit like iron is inhabited by fire: "As iron placed in fire immediately takes on its color, so the fl esh, after having received the vivifying word within, is freed from corruption and clothed in the flesh of Christ" (Cyril of Alexandria). This is a presence of fusion without confusion, of communion, of a carnal reciprocity, a true "blending," according to St. Gregory of Nyssa: "In becoming flesh, the Word has mixed with man and taken unto itself our nature so that the human may be deified by this blending with God: our past is entirely sanctified by Christ" (Against Apollinarius).

This incessant transfusion of divine life within us is the work of the Holy Spirit, the great mystery of His kenosis, of His utter gift of Himself when He breathes into us the presence of the Word with whom He puts us into immediate contact, a contact in every moment. The power of His creative breath penetrates and animates our entire being and our body right into the smallest of our cells. The Holy Spirit has only one "passion," and that is to mold us into the resemblance of Christ!

In this mutual cohabitation, God rests in us corporally (Col. 2:9) and we rest corporally in God. We rest in God because in Him, what can happen to us? A tense body does not express the image of God but witnesses to His absence. It cries out its fear and its solitude; turned in on itself, closed, the divine breath no longer circulates within it. It is a joy to rest physically in God, all doors open, confident, for then we acquire the certitude that God guides us. In turn, He finds in us the possibility of extending His presence infinitely, without obstacle. We wed the movement of incarnation of the Word which plunges into our flesh and renders it always more transparent to Him.

119

This reciprocal interpenetration is an endless growth, an experience always renewed in which the light of God in our consciousness ends by radiating on our face and in our acts, our gestures, our behavior, even in our politics and our model of society, for why would these not also be in the image of God? What other reference could we have to manage our human relations than the relations of the three divine Persons among themselves? "Our social program is the dogma of the Trinity," said Nicholas Fedorov.

In the person who is liberated and inhabited by Christ, the flesh is no longer carnal and magnetized toward the lower; a new corporality forms itself, "so that the life of Jesus may be manifested in our mortal flesh" (2 Cor. 4:11). Christ has become our companion in the flesh, as the Fathers stated. He has sanctified and liberated our flesh, wrote St. Irenaeus (Bishop of Lyons, second century). If not, the soul would be saved but not the whole person. It is, therefore, also the body which is filled, "steeped," with the presence of Christ and of the Holy Spirit. This state assumes, of course, that asceticism does its work of purification, for the passions cover the heart and deliver it to demonic forces that are as vampires and parasites, and who make of the interior temple a den of thieves.

If the body is our "way of being here in the world," it means that our body is not an object but an integral part of who we are — we are our body. In this sense, the body itself becomes a prayer, each time that its way of being here is correct; that is, when it permits contact with being, with depth. Our manner of being here is false each time the body inhibits this contact. In sin, on separation from God, the soul inflates itself with pride, as the Fathers said, and so does the body since it expresses the soul. Rather than being "rooted and founded" (Eph. 3:17) in its depth, it removes itself from it, pulls in the stomach, lifts the breath into the chest, raises the shoulders, and becomes completely uncentered and subject to all the tensions we know so well. There is no physical tension that is not an expression of something unhealthy on the spiritual level.

A prayer which includes the body, for instance, provoking its relaxation, opens it and places it face-to-face with the object of its search. True prayer, that of surrender and confidence, of complete offering of oneself, always instigates a profound relaxation of the body, but in this case the process is much quicker: a perfectly relaxed body is instantly open to the mystery of which it is the temple. Our entire work is to become open: *"Ephphatha"* — open yourself! — said Christ (Mk. 7:34). The key to opening up is to feel through the five senses.

The liturgy, which is indispensable to the Jesus Prayer, has familiarized us with the use of the senses, for all its teaching is built on this experience: seeing the liturgical movements, the color of the ornaments, the gestures, the icons, hearing the chants, smelling the incense, tasting communion, letting oneself be touched by mystery. The five senses are windows opened onto the invisible. The goal is

121

not to interpret the sensation, not to reflect on what our senses perceive, but to simply receive them, to "let oneself be seized" (Phil. 3:13), to "Judge not" (Mt. 7:1). When our senses stop fixing and objectifying, then the distance between that which they feel and the self disappears. We can then descend into the depth of the sensation and "abide" there (Jn. 15:4–15), receiving the sensation in its pure state, bathing in it: to see, to hear, to taste, to enter within, to let oneself go, to experience life there where there are no more images, forms, or appearances.

This attitude of submission and surrender to all that comes to us, relishing each moment through the five senses instead of wanting to master it through exterior domination leads us into the profound silence of being. Through feeling, our listening to the divine becomes carnal. Sensation invades our ordinary consciousness and makes it possible to transcend the mental, to open itself to other levels and to enter little by little, thanks to the prayer, into what the Fathers called the sensation of the divine. This is a "feeling" in the body and the soul of an ineffable presence found in the spirit and capable of seizing our entire being, into the least of our cells. God finally ceases to be a "ghost" for us, we can touch Him and cry out with Gregory Palamas: "Flesh of my flesh, bones of my bones!" We do not find Him in words, even if they are the ones of the Jesus Prayer! "Do not heap up empty phrases!" (Mt. 6:7), says Christ, "Touch Me!" (Lk. 24:39).

If He has indeed come out of "what no eye has seen nor ear heard …," it is precisely to become flesh and to assimilate Himself to us so that we might be "eyewitnesses of His Majesty" (2 Pet. 1:16), "touch with our hands" (1 Jn. 1:1), feel with our whole being, "know Him" (Phil. 3:10).

The Jesus Prayer has as a "goal" to make us completely conformed to Christ even through our "body of misery" (Phil. 3:14 and 21). "Without the spiritual feeling (that is to say, feeling through the body- soul- spirit)," said Gregory the Sinaite, "it is impossible to taste the beatitude of divine things. Through passions which kill our natural powers, we become insensible to the action of the Holy Spirit. For the one who does not hear spiritually, does not see and does not feel, is spiritually dead." Saint Thomas Aquinas wrote: "He is wise who alone tastes things," and St. Clement of Alexandria stated: "We can even sense what God is if we make the effort through all sensation to join the reality of every being, instead of distancing ourselves from it, and penetrate its inmost nature … There we can discover the immensity and holiness of Christ, and progress toward the abyss of His infinity where we may glimpse the Almighty."

This is true "knowing" that opens us to "eternal life" where the important thing is to "feel everything in God" (Isaac the Syrian). We begin by feeling our own body, since we are co-corporal with Christ; through baptism we have plunged into Him and have "put Him on" (Rom. 6:1–11), through the Eucharist we are "assimilated" to Him in the most realistic sense of the word. His flesh becomes ours and it is His blood which flows in our veins (Jn. 6:56).

To be Christ means to look away from ourselves and our weaknesses, forgetting ourselves and looking only at Christ present within us. For Christ lives within us. No matter what we do, He is within us, He is more us than we are ourselves. He is the intelligence of our intelligence, the will of our will, the effort of our effort, the light of our eyes, the word of our mouth, His heart is our heart, His members are our members. All that we do is done by Him. To be conscious of Christ is to live Christ there where we are and in what we are doing now, to feel Him under our skin in a realistic way, to live the least movement of our body and let Christ blossom through every action, every word, every gesture. There is no more me and Him, but Him alone. It no longer matters then that circumstances please or displease us since Christ does what He wants and He comes to us as He chooses. Everything is grace and thanksgiving, joy, union. He is in us and everything speaks to us of Him. We see His trace everywhere.

Unity of life ... simplicity ... eff ort without effort ... This is the discovery of the great law of all spiritual life: the non-action, the relaxation of the will, where it is no longer a matter of doing but of letting be done in and through us what Christ wants to do. This is a coming out of the duality and the progressive death of the ego with its chaotic needs and desires which only lead to suffering. Passive growth or active passivity, it is hard to define what is typical of the attitude of surrender in which we collaborate in a work that is completely beyond us: the unique desire of the unique desired One. As the instrument played by the artist, to use St. Irenaeus' vivid image, I am "lived" by Christ. Christ lives me. Indeed, being an instrument, my life becomes music and play, as opposed to the tensions that secrete the poison of bad asceticism. This is the grace of childhood rediscovered, spiritual Childhood, the song of Being which resonates confidence and openness through letting go.

A new consciousness begins to be born, an unsuspected power completely unknown to the old ego manifests itself and animates us: "the inner man" (Eph. 3:16), "the hidden person of the heart" (1 Pet. 3:16). The more the feeling of the presence interiorizes itself, the more our physical and mental tensions disappear, letting the doors of our inner dwelling open up.

This sensation is like the wave of the sea which can take on all sorts of forms on the exterior. We can feel under our feet the beaten earth or the rock, the flat ground or the unevenness of stones. Our hands can, in contacting things, feel warmth or coldness, and our eyes and ears can define multiple forms. But as the wave is connected to the depth of the ocean, so sensation is also related to the infinity of our interior consciousness if we do not stop at the forms on the surface when our footsteps on something or our hands touch, when our eyes look or our ears hear. The mystery of the presence never ceases to deepen for someone who remains in this transparence of sensation in all things and who works consistently until it becomes second nature.

We find here the great strength of the mystical tradition of Christianity where "faith" does not define itself as an intellectual belief, but comes from evidence lived, from the sensation of the transcendent. "I call experience," said Maximus the Confessor, "the knowing which rises beyond all concept, the participation with the object which reveals itself beyond all thought."

And then one day, after perhaps years of hard work, the breakthrough happens, like a knife piercing through to the depths: the heart is taken, touched, literally inflamed, and Christ reveals Himself. This is a burning "sensation of God" which invades our being body- soul-spirit, but this time from their common center — the heart, which is "the most interior body in the body" (St. Macarius), "the essence of the soul" (St. Nicodemus), "the temple of the spirit" (St. Gregory the Sinaite), "the root of all things" (St. Isaac).

If the heart governs all the organs, then once it is possessed by grace, it reigns over all thoughts and all members (St. Maximus the Confessor). The heart is the center of human existence, the point of convergence of all spiritual, mental and bodily powers, the way through which we come in contact with all that exists (Theophan the Recluse) outside as well as inside. It is there that we encounter

God face-to-face and unite ourselves to Him. It is there only that we are truly face-to-face with our brothers and sisters, and that communion with them is possible.

Christ perfectly human and perfectly God came to live this fullness of unity among us and, in doing so, he offers Himself as the way of return and liberation. To follow Christ fully, "to become Christ," according to the expression of St. Gregory of Nyssa, is realized in the heart. That is where Christ takes shape (Gal. 4:19) and that "we take the form of Christ" (Origen), "that is where the Logos is born like a Child" (St. Clement of Alexandria), and that is where He wants to radiate, in each person who lets Him grow within, the unity of the body, soul and spirit realized through His incarnation (St. Maximus). This growth is a perpetual creation. That is why it is important to descend into the heart to meet God and to become similar to Him in an intimate reciprocity. The way always goes from the periphery toward the axis and as long as we have not reached the incandescent kernel, we are pilgrims. "Outside of the heart, man is without a home, but in his heart he is both at home and with God," says an aphorism of the Fathers.

As much as the "feeling" of the periphery can be like a fleeting wave, so through the awakening of the heart does "the sensation of mystery" become durable and the memory of the presence constant. It is in this "feeling," says Theophan the Recluse, "that resides the beginning of religion ... To be seized by it has a very great importance in the spiritual life. Whoever possesses the feeling lives interiorly." (Feeling as understood here comes from the spirit as opposed to emotion which comes from the soul.) It is not surprising, then, that Theophan calls the heart "the organ of divinization," or "the sense organ for our relation to God," as the contemporary theologian Staniloae clarifies. For the way goes at the same time from the axis to the periphery, and as our tensions fall away, that is to say as our door opens, the entire body becomes a great heart where from then on the most interior sentiment, arising from the Holy of Holies that is the heart, is allied with the most exterior sensation, the place of physical contact with things through the body.

Here are the two important stages in this prayer. The first begins where we are: in the exterior. It is hard work, a concentration of our whole being, based on a decision that creates an existence in which the saints can bring together gigantic energies into a single space and where few things are obtained without "relentlessness" (Th eophan), a perpetual beginning again. Everything in the life of this person, everything without exception, is organized around this goal, making way for the requirement which must come before all other things! Having risen out of confused and contradictory aspirations of our nature, we are conscious of living a decisive choice which determines a type of unity (Eph. 4:13–14), and rectifies our past. This decision, dearly bought, fixes the order of our values and reveals the ultimate meaning of sacrifice, which is to become "obedient until death" (Phil. 2:8). "Beginnings are very important: everything consists of a firm determination not to give oneself any rest until we have attained our goal, at whatever cost, come what may, even if we die on the way or if we lack courage before the trials of the way, even if the world crumbles" (St. Teresa of Avila). The saints are unanimous on this point!

If the first stage begins here where we are, on the exterior, the second stage begins where God is found: in the interior. God only gives Himself completely to someone who also gives himself completely. The heart opens, prayer springs forth and acts from itself. We are involuntarily carried along. There is no more labor. This is the contemplative state, the invading by grace "far more abundantly than all that we ask or think" (Eph. 3:20). In the first stage, God calls and attracts us, inviting us ceaselessly to sacrifice our golden calves. He gives us the capacity to struggle and the oil of the athlete, leads us step by step, picks us up from our falls and maintains us on the right path. He is the effort and the very dynamism of our courage. But the decision belongs entirely to us. It is our free response to the call of God who does not infringe on us at any moment. However, at the very instant in which we, aft er a long effort with this difficult prayer, "seek first the kingdom of God" rather than adding it to the rest of our desires, when our reaching toward the unique has become as real and pure in us as a diamond, then we become virgin and are prepared for the coming of the beloved: the emptying of self calls forth the fullness of the presence. This is the second stage on the way of the prayer.

Virginity always opens itself to fecundity. In the spiritual life, we are mother only if we are virgin. Only pure, undivided hearts will see God. When our whole being has become "yes": "Let it be done to me according to your word" (Lk. 1:38). The covenant is then possible and virginity offers itself to maternity. Christ Himself says it with power: "My mother and My brothers are those who hear the word of God and do it" (Lk. 8:21). He engenders in himself the word, under the power of the Spirit as did Mary, Virgin and Mother. Mary is the archetype of the new man, the "path of return," the open door through which comes the river of mystical theology. She is the beloved of the Song of Songs, pregnant with all the promises of the future, the mother-earth who opens herself to the seed of the Word for an extraordinary fecundity: the birth of a new humanity. Her path toward virginity is such an accomplishment through her years of prayer at the temple that she becomes in her "yes" a mystical table of the first Eucharist, a living altar where her flesh and blood are transformed into the flesh and blood of Christ. In her virginity, Mary offers herself to God; in her maternity God offers Himself to her, and the two in Jesus Christ are co-corporal.

In this second phase of the prayer, we are mother at each moment whatever we do: Christ comes out of our heart and blossoms in all our actions and gestures. We no longer have on one side our thoughts and on the other our behavior. The intellect has descended into the heart. The ideas about God which inhibit our encounter with

Him are now filled with the sensation of the very reality of God manifesting Himself in an immediate presence.

The least thought of God interrupts our direct relationship with Him when the intellect is separated from the heart. On the other hand, when the two are reunited, there is a seizing of the consciousness which then finds itself completely occupied by the experience of God in an intimate reciprocity. God is not in our consciousness as an object, as someone who would be distant from us. Rather, our consciousness fuses with His. It becomes an identity without confusion, a transparence to God in the consciousness of humanity, understanding that consciousness is in the whole body, in our gestures, our movements, our interior silence, "to the ends of our fingertips" as Symeon the New Theologian stated. This consciousness is a continual embracing of fire, a supreme reciprocal inhabitation, where "God experiences man so that man may experience God," according to the saying of the Fathers. In this co-penetration, we are divinized, shimmering with the holiness of God because the Spirit sets us on fi re. This alliance, in which we resemble God more and more, awakens the human person within who is the radiance of the divine presence on our face and in our acts. "To see your face is like seeing the face of God," Jacob said to Esau.

At this stage, the prayer "Lord Jesus Christ, Son of God, have mercy on me, a sinner," has become pure prayer, the prayer of the whole of

131

our being. Over the years, the words have traced a path from the intellect toward the heart, and from there the whole being is projected into God with infinite love. Now the words continue to repeat themselves, engraved in the memory of each cell. Yet these words, even when pronounced, are no longer "work," no longer represent for the intellect an object which has an autonomous existence, since their content is realized. "The Word became flesh ... to all who received Him, who believed in His name, He gave power to become children of God ... and from His fullness have we all received" (Jn. 1:12–16). The words henceforth express in the literal meaning of the word "ex-press:" to press outward, manifesting this reality of the immediate contact with God.

It is then through our very being that we pray, as could be said of St. Francis of Assisi and of St. Seraphim of Sarov who did not pray, but were prayer. The whole being has become the sacrament of what the words contain and promise as seed. When we see a flower, we no longer think of the seed. The words of the prayer are exceeded by experience. The presence of God fills everything, and perhaps someday they will disappear in the intensity of this presence. Th e prophecy of Ezekiel comes true: "A new heart I will give you; and a new spirit I will put within you; and I will take out of your flesh the heart of stone and give you a heart of flesh ... and I will put My Spirit within you" (Ezek. 36:26).

In biblical anthropology, as in the hesychast tradition, the heart and the spirit are the same reality, and are interchangeable. It is the Lord who shapes the spirit of man within him, said Zechariah (Zech. 12:1). The heart-spirit is the principle which unites, illumines, fi lls the soul and the body intimately blended together, one depending on the other. In our human nature, the spirit is that which resembles God the most. As St. John said: "God is Spirit, Light, Love." The Hebrew word *ruah* designates wind, breath, the human spirit, angels, the spirit of God and the Holy Spirit. This indicates the power of our spirit and its affinity with God.

The tragedy of the pagan — and there is a pagan in each one of us — is to confuse the soul with the spirit. This has been the drama of the west for many centuries which is now leading to the decay of civilization, culture and art.

If human beings have no spirit, the duality body- soul closes us within ourselves, makes us the center of the world, and no profound unity is possible. We seek to escape, either by dominating matter, by seeking immortality of the body or by trying to conquer the world. This can range from taking aspirin and tranquilizers, to interplanetary travel, to studying all the current forms of consciousness expansion. The person who does not know that he has a spirit can only be unhappy; he finds himself at an impasse. There is no way out from any of his problems, and even when joy presents itself he does not know what to do with it. We are a path of development toward ourselves and toward God. If we do not know our identity, we find ourselves in darkness, the opposite of deification; our life is a puzzle that leads us nowhere, and we do not know the why or the how. That is why the Bible is as much revelation of man as revelation of God! The last century ended with Nietzsche's statement: "God is dead!" and our century may end with: "Man is dead!" Get rid of the source today and tomorrow the stream will dry up.

If the Gospel is "good news," such a cry of joy from beginning to end, it is because in revealing human beings to themselves, it offers us at the same time the possibility of experiencing God within ourselves here and now! The entire evangelical message is revelation of the heart-spirit. Faith is, therefore, not a belief of the soul, an intellectual and external adherence to truths which will hypothetically realize themselves after our death, but the experience of our own mystery, our life, the source of all life. To have faith is simply to live, to live fully. Not to have faith is to be delivered to nothingness, which is hell. It is extraordinary to see with how much clarity Christ expresses Himself on this subject: "My soul is very sorrowful," He said (Mt. 26:38) and "Father, into Your hands I commit My Spirit" (Lk. 23:46).

In the same way Mary says in the Magnificat: "My soul magnifies the Lord, and my spirit rejoices in God my Savior" (Lk. 1:46–47).

The "soul," from the Greek psyche, is our psychology with its great instruments: intelligence, will, affection, imagination. The soul animates the body, lives in its intimacy, vibrates, smells, sees, thinks. Since the division introduced into humanity by the fall, it is multiple, agitated, changing, conditioned: today good humor, tomorrow bad mood, "this pleases me, this displeases me ... I am attracted or repulsed." The soul is constantly tossed about by its states, tyrannized by its emotions, continually delivered as a victim to any event from the outside, conditioned and truly slave of exterior conditions, circumstances, encounters, problems. Because we live only in the soul, we have become "people with problems." But the soul is so united to the body that it is also affected by it. We only have to have a toothache or stomachache to be in a bad mood.

But in God's plan, the most utilized image by the Fathers to defi ne the relationship between the body and the soul, is the one of the artist and his instrument. The body is the instrument of the soul, it is formed and animated by it. It is through the soul, says Irenaeus, that the body receives its growth and structure. The soul possesses the body and reigns over it. It is, therefore, its mission to lead the body into its proper spiritualization- deification. The soul is on the border between matter and spirit, which is the reason for its awesome importance. Gregory of Nyssa states that if the soul turns toward the spirit, it spiritualizes itself; if it turns toward the flesh it materializes itself. The soul purified of its passions and possessed by the Holy Spirit becomes itself spirit, said St. Macarius. Then it is all light, entirely penetrated by light, fusing with God, and in that act, the body equally spiritualizes and deifies itself. This is the very purpose of the prayer!

Our soul can be in the depths of mortal anguish, physical trials and terrible psychic troubles, but whatever hell we may be going through, we can feel a deeper place, like a tiny space of peace, of relaxation and hope, a loving source of joy, or a simple glow. It reveals itself when we truly accept the trial to its end. It is there that is found "the narrow way" of which Christ speaks, the light in the depths of our darkness. That is the heart-spirit in us, always present, but we only rarely go there, if at all! In any case we experience the difference between the soul and the spirit when there is coexistence within us of a storm or trouble and at the same time of a profound calm. The characteristics of the heart-spirit are peace, joy, love.

The Fathers said that we human beings are a microcosm: we contain within the cosmos, its structure and its laws. Therefore, "to become conscious of the relationships between the spirit, the soul and the body, we can compare them to the relationships between the sun, the moon and the earth. The sun is compared to the spirit, the moon to the soul, and the earth to the body. In the same way that the earth goes around the sun, the body gravitates around the spirit. The soul is a satellite of our body, its light comes from the sun-spirit." As the moon receives and reflects the solar light, but rotates around the earth to which it is linked, so the soul receives the light –of the spirit and transmits it to the body around which it turns. The earth orbits around the sun from which it receives the light of day: from the moon, it receives nocturnal light; thus the body orbits around the spirit as around its original center which enlightens it, being light of the full consciousness, and nocturnal light, which is a luminous reflection of the unconscious. The sun (the spirit) is the spiritual center which illumines the earth and the moon (the body and the soul).

But then we may ask what is this "heart- spirit" which our prayer must awaken? Every verbal approach will leave us hungry. It is the dimension of transcendence, the beyond in our depths, outside of space and time, unconditioned, that within us which is consciousness, receptivity, and finally mystery; not "what we cannot understand" but, on the contrary, that which we have never finished understanding, for we constantly experience a new aspect of its Life.

The spirit comes from God as the stream from its source, it is our umbilical cord from which we receive continually. But that translates only one aspect of reality. If the words "source" or "umbilical cord" denote a distance, they are the wrong words. The spirit is literally penetrated by divine presence, to such an extent that it is diffi cult sometimes in reading St. Paul to know whether he is speaking of the human spirit or of the Holy Spirit. This is also true of the Fathers. But we know through ourselves also for we cannot easily distinguish within us the presence of our spirit and the presence of God. Our spirit is completely seized by divine light. Its mode of awareness is not like the intelligence of the soul which operates by deduction, reflection, analysis, synthesis; the spirit knows by being seized even before we have formulated anything. It is the interior look, c ontemplative, filled with wonder.

The spirit sees, it operates through vision, which is why one of its characteristics is light. It is illumined when it sees. When it lives only through God, it is attracted above all by the splendor of God and the splendor of glorified creation which is His reflection. It is fascinated by beauty. True beauty always gives direct access to the heart-spirit. That is why the criterion of authenticity of beauty is the joy which is the fruit of the spirit, durable, indelible joy as only the spirit can give, not a passing emotion of the soul.

Beauty is the face of God. Psalm 45 says of Christ: "You are the fairest of the sons of men." But Christ is "the effigy of the Father," as St. Paul reminds us, and the Holy Spirit is His splendor. And if our spirit is sensitive to splendor, it is because such beauty inhabits it and is its substance. Our spirit can be seized by splendor in relation to everything: a countryside, a work of art, an encounter with another person … And, little by little, as the spirit opens, this look becomes constant and no longer loses the trace of Being found in all things, this "diaphany" of God which the specialists of the sacred call "the numinous" and the Fathers call "the flame of things." All the teachings on the icons are there to awaken us to this look, but the Jesus Prayer placed upon beings and things makes of the whole of creation an immense temple in which humanity celebrates a cosmic liturgy. Priests of creation, we decipher the world through our prayers and transform it into eucharistic bread. Everything can off er itself as sacrament of the divine presence, and we make our way through life "as though we saw the invisible" (Heb. 11:27). In this experience, prayer goes from our heart to the heart of things. Then the face of beauty at the heart of all that touches us, shakes us and opens us to our own being sends us back to our image within: the heart-spirit.

It is the heart-spirit which is truly the image of God and infuses it into the soul and the body to nourish them. The true identity of our spirit, of our heart is there. When we first approach it, it is silence; an abyss of silence reveals itself to the one whose prayer has quieted the agitations of the soul and of the body. But this silence is also the source which gives life, which engenders and expresses itself. This is the second characteristic of the heart-spirit: it is manifestation, expression, word. And this life is energy, movement, breath — this is the third characteristic. The heart-spirit is in the image of its divine archetype: image of the Father — source of life, image of the Christ — Word, image of the Holy Spirit — energy-breath. "In man there is a Nous, Logos and Pneuma," said Gregory the Sinaite, "but the Nous does not exist without the Word nor the Word without the Pneuma, always one is in the other and each for itself. The Nous expresses itself through the Word and the Word manifests itself through the Pneuma. Thus we carry within the reflection of the inexpressible and archetypal Trinity, revealing that our spirit is created in the image of God. Th e Nous — the Father, the Logos — the Son, the Holy Spirit

— the Pneuma, this is what the Fathers, illumined by God, teach us about the unique God revealing Himself in three."

We have the concrete experience of this reality within us and around us. All that we see is enveloped by silence, letting us guess behind its existence the mysterious source of its life, and all that we see is form, manifestation, flesh of the word, everything is fi lled with energy and movement. Everywhere all is trinitarian presence. But it is in breathing that this experience is the most realistic: there is nothing more intimate to God and to humanity than the breath, and that is where this osmosis is strongest.

"Then the Lord breathed into his nostrils the breath of life; and man became a living being" (Gen. 2:7). This is the creative act par excellence which the resurrected Christ will reiterate at the new creation: "He breathed upon them" (Jn. 20:22), a gesture which the priest renews on each baptized person who is born to the true life.

Breathing is the great movement of life, not only in its birth but also in its continual metamorphosis within us. To become conscious of this in prayer which connects the word to the breath makes our way of breathing a way of transparence to mystery.

This "breath of life," which God breathes into us constantly, is our spirit and inseparably His life as Father-Son-Holy Spirit. We are, therefore, not only a passive temple of the Trinitarian presence, but also animated, vivified, maintained in existence by the divine Trinity at all times. As is stated in Psalm 104: "When Thou sendest forth Thy Spirit, they are created; when Thou takest away their breath, they die and return to their dust." Therefore, "to live is Christ," says St. Paul, that is to say, always the whole of Christ: effigy of the Father — splendor of the Spirit. To live is to be in communion with the three divine Persons and the consciousness of their presence opens us to our spirit and transforms us: their image in us resembles us more and more — it is our slow deification. A person is truly a person only if he or she becomes God. This is the birth of the person within, an undefinable mystery which both unifies our body- soul- spirit and leads them to their transmutation toward God.

At this juncture we receive our true face, the "mask" of Christ, and bear His divine traits. In this amazing communion resides the ultimate depth of the Jesus Prayer which is none other than creation continuing onward, the creation of the person. Only God is truly Person and humans can only become persons through the divine Person. This communion-osmosis, in which the face of Christ shines through ours, gives us existence and form. Without this deification, we have no face, since we truly exist only through participation in the face of God, only through this "co-being." Otherwise our face is formless chaos, absence or "mask of the beast" (Gregory of Nyssa).

This consciousness never ceases to deepen; to rediscover it as much as possible and maintain it as long as possible through our daily

existence is the path of the spiritual life. There is none other. Th is
consciousness slowly illuminates the soul and body with the holiness
of God. This divine-human reciprocity is a dialogical alliance of my
"I" with the divine "Thou." And this incessant interior dialogue will
inscribe itself bit by bit in every exterior relationship with beings and
things. At the heart of every encounter between two persons, there is
the great "Third One."

If "God is love," as St. John reveals (1 Jn. 4:8), then we too are love!
"That they may all be one, even as Thou, Father, art in Me, and I
in Thee, that they also may be in Us, so that the world may believe
that Thou hast sent Me" (Jn. 17:21). That is the Church, and as such,
says Maximus the Confessor, she is the "icon of God" on earth. Th e
first Christians lived it that way. The Acts of the Apostles states that
they were "but one heart and one soul" and "placed everything in
common" (Acts 4:32). This resemblance with God goes to the extent
of the complete gift of self as He did on the cross, for "there is no
greater love than to lay one's life down for one's friend" (Jn. 15:16).
But in this act of surrender in which we apparently die, empty and
sacrifice ourselves, we are actually born into our true identity,
opening to our spirit, awakening to our unique and free personhood,
and finally knowing our true mystery.

Sin, on the other hand, consists of not praying; that is, in turning
away from God or in living as though He did not exist. Our spirit is

then separated from God, from its origin (the root of the words "original sin"). Our soul is no longer fed, having lost its source. This leads to the great laceration within us, to our fall, whether sudden or progressive: the spirit famished for God rushes into the soul to nourish itself and feeds on it by its absolute need. That is when we truly die. Original sin is mortal; this is our state, we commit it constantly. The other sins are only bubbles which rise to the surface of a water whose depths are polluted by our separation from God. The soul weighed down by the spirit and no longer being nourished by it, will seek its nourishment from the body, which is then fed on in turn. The soul becomes carnal and wears out the body and the latter falls into illness and death, because it does not receive the spiritual life of the soul: this is the birth of the "carnal man." His body and soul are burned by an absolute thirst for the spirit which inhabits them. Instead of rejoicing in God, they seek external pleasures and are literally hypnotized by the world.

Banished to the exterior world, "extrodetermined" say the sociologists, living in a consciousness completely turned away from our spirit, we enjoy things as ends in themselves, an act in which the soul becomes satisfied with itself and concentrates on its own pleasure. It inflates itself, says St. Augustine: to the absence of God it substitutes an obsession with itself, and the impulse toward adoration rising from our depths is reduced to autoidolatry and to a conscious or unconscious idolatry of everything around us. It absolutizes the relative and attaches itself in an infinite way to the finite, becoming both chained and manipulated.

Persons who have lost their dimension of the heart-spirit, no longer feeding on the unique desire for the unique desired One, are projected outward toward other sources, other relationships in the duality and multiplicity of desires. This is an affirmation of a double self, the caricature of the image of God, a pride that eliminates God and makes of a human being another Lucifer. This is the perversion of the will, a will to independence which is the "principle and mother of all the passions" (Theophan the Recluse). Decomposition begins, disintegrating our being until hate and death have the last word. At the end of the passions, there is only the void; in place of the silence of the spirit, of the source of life which is the Father, there is anguish before suffering and death, with the compensation of pleasure in all its forms; in place of light which the Word gives to our consciousness, we fi nd the darkness of meaninglessness and of the absurdity of life and seek compensation in acquiring possessions; in place of the vivifying Holy Spirit whose powerful energies communicate love, we find the incommunicability and horror of solitude, with the compensation of the search for power and domination. The anguish of death, the absurdity of life and solitude are the void of the person whose spirit no longer has God as host. This makes of us wanderers never satisfied, insane persons who no longer know who they are, sickly people who heal only our symptoms because we no longer know the cause of our distress.

A society of consumption exploits marvelously this frantic multiplicity of our desires. But after years of running to satisfy our appetites without managing to do so, we notice that there is still an emptiness within, an inexplicable desire, a longing for something unknown. And as soon as we take this yearning seriously, our true maturity begins.

Because nothing exterior or physical has been able to satisfy this yearning, we learn that it is metaphysical, a call from the beyond within, a cry from Being, the last remnants of an experience of God within us who ceaselessly cries out: "Adam, where are you?"

It is precisely in this void, in this yearning, so well described by the starets Silouan and which is none other than the groaning of the spirit, that the Jesus Prayer will take root. Listening to this call from the depths is already the beginning of the prayer and its foundation: "Hear, O Israel!" The return begins in this way, and the name of Jesus, like the Good Samaritan on the side of the road, will one by one heal our wounds opened by separation and alienation.

Chapter Five
THE PATH OF CONVERSION
AND ASCETICISM

A new heart I will give you, and a new spirit I will put within
you; and I will take out of your flesh the heart of stone and give
you a heart of flesh.
Ezekiel 36:26

What must we do on the path of return? That is our question! It
was also the question which John the Baptist asked himself (Lk.
3:10). John the Baptist is at the crossroads of universal history and of
our most personal history. He is the annunciating prophet of the new
times, if we accept to "lay the axe to the root of the tree" (Lk. 3:8–9)
and take the way of return, or conversion. For the "tree" is our heart-
spirit and it is the "root" which is subtly infiltrated by pride and love
of self which are the source of all passions. We are then to "put to
death the snake who nests and murders beneath the spirit" (Pseudo-
Macarius). Here the love of God and of others is the only remedy:
"He who has two coats, let him share with him who has none; and he
who has food, let him do likewise" (Lk. 3:11).

Rediscovering that which unifies us, rediscovering our fi rst innocence leads us to become one with God to such an extent that there is no longer the consciousness within us of a differentiated self, distinct from God. All that we know then is love, nothing else: the unique desire for the unique desired One which makes of life a communion of love with the Creator and with all that He endlessly creates at each moment.

The opposite is our propulsion toward the exterior which kindles the multiplicity of desires and makes of life only hatred and division: "We devour ourselves reciprocally like serpents. Th e communion of love is replaced by the hidden fear of death, and this death," says Maximus the Confessor, "is the cause of our turning love into destructive passions." The self is so closed in upon itself by this metaphysical anguish that the other, including God, is always, even unconsciously, a potential enemy.

In a person whose spirit is cut off from God, the soul enters into a radical change of perspective and passes into a state of dualism. Instead of living through God, of seeing in His light and with His eyes, the soul sees and lives through the self in an autonomous way. This is a false self, non-being, the empirical existence where each act of affi rmation of the self increases the dualistic tension between the self and God, between the self and others. And as the self depends upon things to affirm it, the ditch never ceases to be dug and God Himself becomes an antagonistic and hostile being, a rival. Little by little all relationships are falsified: with oneself, with others, with God, with the whole of creation. This ontological denaturation brings to life in us a sort of predisposition to bad faith, where we constantly try to make things other than what they are, so that they serve our appetite for pleasure and power and our arbitrary impulses in every moment. This is the "noisy tumult of the passions" according to the patristic expression, the opposite of interior silence, of hesychia.

Here is the beginning of all decay. Our existence is fractured and we plunge into internal contradictions that can only make us suffer. A person who persists in walking with a broken leg will only suffer; and every desire comes out of this deep fracture which we carry within and which inevitably brings us to tragedy. The great significance of true asceticism is found here: in discerning the motives behind our way of being and acting.

Where does my desire come from and where is it going? That is the ground of asceticism, its primary matter, and the very place of our penitence. Asceticism is a guardian over every interior and exterior movement. Nothing is possible — no accomplishment, no happiness, no peace — as long as desire is turned in upon itself, egocentric and greedy! There is no spiritual way or prayer which can be maintained without battling these passionate desires. The Fathers are unanimous on this point. Love itself can only be born when the self renounces its pretension to absolute autonomy.

Orthodox spirituality understands by the word "passion" all the egocentric desires through which the demon seeks to capture human beings. But the tradition, particularly Evagrius (fourth century), summarizes this turmoil in our psyche into eight common denominators. This is a precious tool of discernment that we must know in its most subtle workings, not only to track the demons that inhabit us, but especially to decipher their hidden way of ambushing us. This criteria allows us on the one hand to habitually stop and look clearly upon our life, entering into repentance, and on the other hand to exercise this observation in a vigilance that becomes permanent with the help of continual prayer.

"He who sees his sin is greater than he who resurrects the dead" (Isaac the Syrian). This is not a matter of judging, but of recognizing evil in order to avoid it. The passions are not destroyed in this inner work, but their powerful dispersed energy are rechanneled toward God.

Prayer and asceticism enter here into a perfect synergy for a common work: the watch of the heart. This state of critical vigilance is an almost continuous state of grace in which we are seeking out the least.

1 Gluttony

The giants of asceticism in the tradition have put gluttony at the head of the passions because it is not merely laughable emories of our childhood, although certain adult behaviors manifest a real fixation with the "oral stage" and the traumatisms experienced in the moment of weaning may leave durable scars or places of regression within them. This is the phenomenon of compensation through eating, inhabited by all the unconscious impulses. Without denying this, it is necessary to go further than early infancy and to integrate all the evils that rise out of it later on.

The Fathers see a very close relationship between the spiritual life and food. John Cassian, Maximus the Confessor, and many others, show that the quality and the quantity of food entering with the mixture of liquids into the body exercise a direct effect on our thoughts. Today science confirms the experience of the ascetics.

The fundamental need for nutrition requires each person to enter into contact with the cosmos, and to take seriously the importance of the body which is intimately linked to it. To observe our way of eating is, therefore, extremely revealing. The passion is not found in the need to eat, but in the capacity of that urge to completely besiege our consciousness and overwhelm it to the point that there is no more room for God. To eat is a test which reveals to what extent we are capable of distancing ourselves from our need for security and our deep anguishes, from our love of self and our solitary pleasures, so that we can be free for God.

That is why the first demonic temptation, which is at the origin of everything, even at the foundation of creation — the one which perverts the creative intention and makes us miss the meaning of life and our true being — is the act of eating, or more precisely, our way of eating. This temptation has dragged humanity into the fall from the beginning of creation (Gen. 3) and, on the other hand, has made it possible for Christ to lift us into a new creation (Mt. 4). We waver at each moment between these two possibilities. We do not eat merely at the table! We are what we eat, we live only through eating, we eat constantly. Indeed, we are beings who are hungry and the entire Bible presents humanity as such. The whole world is our food, and our body is of the same matter as the world: this osmosis is, therefore, direct and without intermediary. God offers us the universe like a table at a universal banquet (Gen. 1:29) and to live is nothing other than to eat! Even Jesus compares His Kingdom to a wedding meal "so that you may eat and drink at my table" (Lk. 22:30), and it is at the wedding at Cana that He manifests His glory for the first time in the act of eating and drinking! (Jn. 4).

We eat with the mouth, but also with our looking, listening, smelling, touching. There is not a moment in the day when we are not in a state of receptivity, and during the night, sleep is still nutrition! Above all, that which envelops, upholds, and penetrates everything, is the breath: if it were possible to suspend all eating for a period of time, we would still have to breathe. It is a matter of life and death.

Why did God create us that way? He could have done it differently. What does this incredible dependence, this continual hunger in relation to the world mean? It means that humanity hungers for God.

152

God is love, and He has made us in His image; that is, for an uninterrupted communion with Him. All that we are and all that surrounds us was created only for that purpose. Creation is a gift from God. In it He gives Himself and reveals Himself; our food is the very life of God, the divine love which offers itself to us in each moment without exception. And our five senses are "open windows" on this invisible presence which awaits us and seeks us, which "breathes into us His breath of life." Thus our multiplicity of desires contains the unique desire for God, and our heart will rest only when it will have found Him, as St. Augustine said.

Behind all the hungers of our life there is God. It is simply for a story of love that God created the world, and without love there is no story at all, only chaos and death. We commune, then, with that which is incapable of giving us life; without God, we commune with death itself.

To become conscious of the presence of God everywhere and in all things, and to become united with God by assimilating Him through this constant nutrition was the original role of human beings who then became priests of creation. Their lives were to be a Eucharist where everything transformed itself into the life of God. Gluttony, which we diabolically reduce to mere child's play, is, therefore, the tragic perversion of this grandiose perspective. We are always either in a state of communion and alliance with God, or in a state of separation from Him. This is original sin: life could have been the "fruit" of an encounter, but we make it an object of consumption.

The ascetic healing of this deviation can only be found in the act of eating correctly. "Eating can be saintliness itself if we eat with gratitude, freeing the sparks of the divine presence, of the Shekinah, which are found in food," said Martin Buber. That is why this apprenticeship is done through three fundamental realities which restore us in Christ, "the living bread which came down from heaven" (Jn. 6:51): the Jesus Prayer, which we "chew" as an actual eating of the word of God; the Eucharist, because "he who eats My flesh and drinks My blood has eternal life" (Jn. 6:54) and can rediscover anew the sacrament of His presence in all food; fasting, through which is revealed to us in a luminous way that our hunger is a hunger for God, for in ceasing to react "normally" to the needs of the flesh, fasting removes from it the poison of that misuse and makes it transparent to the radiance of the One who lives within it. An offertory from the ancient liturgy of the Gauls which has been restored by the Orthodox Church of France states: "May all flesh be silent and the King of glory will enter it."

2 Lewdness.
The background which weaves the fabric of gluttony is also that of the other passions. Humanity can be pictured as an enormous spider, a stomach with eight arms, which ceaselessly, throughout its life, brings everything toward its center — the self. Lewdness is, according to the Fathers, the direct result of too much food (St. John Cassian). But, as in the case with eating, sexuality is a

"structure" of humanity, living and expressing itself through us. At its basis is a yearning for the lost unity and the search, never fully satisfied, for our feminine or masculine side. These two realities are the very foundation of any spiritual path, and that is why chastity is for the monk, as for married persons, a foundation stone on which our being will grow.

For those who do not have a strong spiritual life, the parasitic soul inhabited by the absolute of the spirit that does not feed itself enough of God, literally ravages the body which inflames itself with longing. The divine fire within us turned away from God becomes a carnal fire and every relationship then becomes pornographic instead of being an epiphany, a cup which opens itself to the visitation of God. The totality of our energy is polarized at the level of genital impulses which submerge our consciousness and fi nd their outlet in the exploitation of another person through thought and imagination, through the concupiscent look, through the violent and egotistical gesture, through the uncontrolled and burning desire, or the solitary pleasure. The body, that temple of our alliance with God, becomes a place of mutual destruction, an object of consumption where all mystery is evacuated. The heart becomes opaque and inaccessible to all other presence besides the demonic.

The only remedy is to let oneself love, to become conscious of the great love of God for us, and that suffi ces to have access to holiness. This is the very meaning of the Jesus Prayer, and it can create marvels. Since sexuality has its seat in the brain, the invocation of the holy name comes to substitute itself for obsessive thought and predisposes the heart to love. This growing love opens the heart-spirit to God and pulls it away from feeding off the soul. Thus liberated, the soul turns itself toward the spirit, and the body turns toward the soul: its liberation is such that love "changes the very substance of things," according to St. John Chrysostom. Our whole being enters into a new tension, the perverted hierarchy body- soul-spirit realigns itself in this process of conversion and unifies itself to the spirit.

It is this becoming which we call chastity, from the Greek *sophrosyne*: plenitude of wisdom. This is not a matter of not loving, of "abstinence," but on the contrary, of a growth of love. "The sexual act, in its soul and truth," says Basil Rozanov, a contemporary Russian philosopher, "is precisely the act through which we do not destroy chastity, but acquire it." The true lover knows how much he is liberated from sexual obsession, as though by enchantment, and that is the well-known test of the authenticity of his love!

True love is a manifestation of the heart- spirit which has no sexual structure, for it is that within us which transcends space and time. Through virginity- chastity, it leads the soul and the body into this same transparence which opens us to a complete shift of aims in all relationships, particularly in sexual ones.

The aim of the monk, of the bachelor and of the couple is the same, but it realizes itself through different paths. For the monk, it is a matter of living the ministry of ultimate things through the most radical rejection of all compromise or of the risk of conformity with the confusions of this world; he retires from it and faces the demons to combat them. His life is both a martyrdom and an immediate celebration of the wedding of the lamb.

The couple live in the midst of the world and celebrate the ministry of the first things, making of daily life the very material of their sacrifice. Marriage then becomes a prophetic image of the coming kingdom. They construct the "House of God," as Clement of Alexandria called it, and constitute the mystery of the Church: the water is changed into wine, daily life is transmuted into its true reality. They enter into an immense metamorphosis. Chastity takes marriage out of its biological fatality and makes of it a spiritual path that presupposes a struggle and an asceticism which matches that of the monks!

There is no love without the cross: the heart of one person is the altar where the other accepts to die. The fruit of this complete union, of this "co-being" which brings an intensely mystical character to the sexual act, is not the birth of a child but the rebirth of the lovers on an always deeper level, a reciprocal begetting. The lover is a contemplative, the sacrament allows him to see the glory of God in the beloved and the Jesus Prayer makes it possible to name her or him. For the one who truly loves, conjugal life manifests itself as a burning bush where God lets Himself be seen, touched, heard.

Lewdness, in solitude or with another, is a hell in which we only see ourselves, as in a labyrinth of mirrors. I only see myself, nothing but myself, to the point of nausea. The demonic bewitching of this deadly passion can only be conquered by the prayer as it becomes continuous, and interior vigilance which awakens us to the movement toward others, teaching us to say: "You!" in an infi nite tenderness where all egocentricity disappears.

3 Avarice. A direct outcome of the two preceding passions, avarice gives them an exterior foundation. Our being closes itself in on some foreign body, and identifies itself with it to such a point, that to lose it is to lose oneself. Evagrius said that the source of avarice is fear. Gluttony and lewdness do not suffice for the pathological need for security; from them is born a permanent dissatisfaction and an instability which plunges the miser into activism. He leaves prayer behind because he has confidence only in himself and in the goods he amasses. His time is planned without the advice of the Holy Spirit and he would be the first to be surprised to learn that the future belongs to God alone. If any prayer is left at all, it is only as insurance on life or to lay out his desires before heaven: "I fast twice a week, I give tithes of all that I get" (Lk. 18:11). The many merits that he has gathered give him a right over God and he feels that he is not far from getting his hands on Him as well.

158

This Pharisee is a hypocrite and a traitor, for he is utterly capable of justifying his attitude: he amasses so as not to depend on anyone. This also justifies his impulse to step into the abyss of pride.

Avarice is so dangerous because it knows no limits: each satisfaction stimulates new desires. This can go from the ridiculous attachment to an eraser, according to the story of a monk told by John Cassian, to the desire to become a bishop and be covered with purple and surrounded with wealth. It does not matter what the thickness of the string holding the bird may be: whether a piece of sewing thread or a heavy rope, it will not be able to fly. This magnificent image from St. John of the Cross confirms the thought of the ascetic Fathers who saw in avarice the symptom of a serious illness in the soul arising from the hardening of the spirit, luke-warmness in the love of God, a lack of courage and an imprisonment in the world of things.

The unconscious roots of the behavior are not to be found in the anal stage any more than gluttony is to be found in the oral stage, as certain psychologists suggest. These are only stages of fixation of a much deeper evil! Having lost reality, we turn toward the shadow: cut off from Life, we seek the substitutes, our driving force no longer being vital dynamism but fear of death. We then believe that we live while, in fact, we only live through appearances and illusion!

"There where your treasure is, so also is your heart." These words of Christ place the knife at the most sensitive spot of the miser. It is "either this or that" and "who is not for Me is against Me"! (Mt. 12:30). As long as a decision to seek the kingdom is not the foundation of human existence, the heart remains divided and the demons besiege it. That is why the Prayer of the Heart, in purifying us, reveals first of all where our treasure is. Abraham's unique treasure was Isaac, his son, whom he offered in sacrifi ce and thereby became the father of all believers (Gen. 22). There is no other answer than his to the call of God: "Here I am!" But first we must ask: What is my Isaac? Where are my preferences? The call to poverty and self-emptying resounds through the whole Bible. It is the very depths of the covenant because our only "Good" is Christ. It is said in the beatitudes of the one who is "poor" and has a "pure heart" that he is doubly "happy": beyond the earthly pleasures, the joy of the "Kingdom of Heaven" opens to him and "he will see God" (Mt. 5:3).

When a person is possessed by nothing other than God Himself, he enters naked into the world and that is the manger; he leaves it naked and that is the cross; in between the two "there is nowhere to lay his head" (Mt. 8:20). In this being, God and humanity are perfectly one: this depends on Christ, but also on the condition of the disciple and of his path which the Jesus Prayer will trace.

The spiritual journey is one of inner liberty and independence of spirit in relation to all things, a freedom without which there is no pure prayer. This space of liberty enters the spirit, restoring the

160

capacity to love things as gifts from God and, as St. Paul says, "deal with the world as though they had no dealings with it" (1 Cor. 7:31). The one who possesses that liberty is master of the world: he entrusts his worries to God and receives from His hands all that happens to him.

4 Sadness

All the passions lead to sadness: it is the great sign of a person detached from God. This is not a matter of a negative psychological temperament, but of a kind of possession of the subconscious depths of the heart which fill themselves with bitterness. The absolute and unquenchable thirst of hell emerges in the little self through the non-satisfaction of desires, impulses, instinctive longings.

A grasping of the finite cannot fulfill an infinite desire, a joy can never last forever if it depends on external things which are changing and temporary by definition! Frustrated in the extreme, this person falls into the inflation of his desires and sees his unhappiness close in upon him in a vicious circle. His sadness is heavy, dragging him down, keeping him from contemplation and purity of heart, and even from spiritual reading. The soul is eaten up by sadness as by ticks, it becomes incapable of being a temple of God and of receiving the Holy Spirit. This failure of human destiny leads directly to a hellish despair, whose impatience and aggression are only external symptoms. This kind of sadness is demonic!

The diagnosis is even easier to see when we consider the fundamental attitude of Christianity: joy. This is the tonality of the Christian, and he is out of tune when unhappy! Gospel means "good news": Christ is Resurrected, and Orthodoxy considers with Isaac the Syrian that there is no greater sin than to be insensitive to that, nor a more terrible betrayal for a disciple than to be without joy. For to be in Christ is to be in joy: "That My joy may be in you, and that your joy may be full" (Jn. 15:11). And because there is no better sign, the Gospel makes of it a commandment! We can cheat with love, but we cannot with joy: only that which is real and authentic has the power to give joy. It is in itself a witness that our God is the living and true God and that we are on the spiritual path. The ancients knew this, and other traditions repeat it: joy is the law of spiritual progress, the great characteristic of the spirit. "Be happy, be perfect," said St. Paul, for without joy there is no holiness; indeed, St. Thérèse of Lisieux added: "A saint who is sad is a sad saint!"

Joy is the sacrament of love, its flower and radiance. Where there is no joy, there is no love either. That is why joy is our unique vocation, since it is the criterion of truth. We are called to it: "Rejoice in the Lord always; again I say: Rejoice!" (Phil. 4:4). Joy is not to be defi ned, we must enter into it: "Enter into the joy of your Master!" (Mt. 25:21).

So sadness, that emanation of all the passions, invites us to an asceticism of the practice of joy. The Fathers say that joy is a great act, for it is the highest act of detachment from the self, the most opposed to egoism, dissolving the darkness of our miseries. It is truly seen only in those for whom "to live is Christ" (Phil. 1:21) and who, through prayer, experience a permanent contemplation of His face. This joy cannot be taken away from us, for it depends on nothing other than He who inhabits our depths.

5 Anger

From a healthy and balanced temperament emanates a
pleasant warmth, but when pricked by circumstances, it becomes scorching with an anger that "boils the blood" as Evagrius says. Th is colossal energy is neutral at fi rst. That is why there can be "saintly" indignation before an injustice, but the one who is in that kind of anger has chosen to place himself in it, remains free and does not let himself be invaded by hatred.

This is completely different from anger which is directed toward someone or something: it perverts itself into negative energy and becomes one of the most dangerous passions. We are then "beside ourselves" as our breath is cut off, and we lose ourselves, become disfigured, even physically and, as Evagrius insists, resemble a demon for we are indeed possessed! John Cassian said that anger darkens the inner sun, destroys discernment, contemplation and all wisdom, for "nothing so much as anger opposes the coming within us of the Spirit." The angry person does not live in the depths of the heart;

established in his exterior nature, he is extremely fragile: the least push is an assault on his self which is always upset, susceptible and suspicious. He is a snow-capped volcano whose risk of eruptions is measured by the size of his ego.

The origin of this disaster is found in the profound dissatisfaction of our being which is unable to blossom. Such a person is in continual aggression against himself and others. Irritability or resentment incessantly gnaw at him and are the symptoms of something else which is undigested. So the organs of digestion — the liver, the gallbladder, the stomach — can be ravaged by it. Even at night this person will find no rest. How much insomnia could be avoided if we considered its spiritual causes! This is also true for all other illnesses because every sickness proper to humanity has a spiritual origin.

The Fathers said that we can only vanquish anger by attacking its roots through an inner transformation of ourselves. The goal of such a transformation is the blessedness of "gentleness," the opposite of anger. But "gentleness" here does not mean passivity or soft ness. Monseigneur Jean de Saint-Denis states that gentleness "consists of being happy in the worst of trials, confessing joy against all evidence and feelings, using joy like a stick to whip sadness, answering our brothers and sisters and every event with joy." As much as anger can destroy the world and ourselves, so can this joy be its true conquest.

Here joy and love are inseparable and point to the Master of the spirit who has dominion over the soul and the body!

The person who is possessed by anger is faced with a great conversion for he is called to love his enemies. This forgiveness is the height of love. The person who does not forgive must stop all practice of the Jesus Prayer because he prays for his own condemnation! Without forgiveness, there is no healing, neither physical nor psychic. Today many doctors are recognizing this. But to forgive does not mean to replace anger or hatred with a tender love for the enemy. Who could manage such an attitude?

To forgive the other is to wish him well from within. Th e greatest good which can come upon someone is the benediction of God. "Love your enemies and pray for those who persecute you," says Christ. This is true forgiveness, rendering good for evil and blessing rather than judging. "Lord, be blessed in this person ..." repeating it until the words on our lips become our interior truth under the action of grace. For ultimately, it is God who forgives through our availability to do it.

This receiving power of God's forgiveness, of His benediction of the other, must descend in us right into the depths of our subconscious, there where our traumas lie. Th e conflict may be ancient and the roots of our hatred are often forgotten or unknown. The subconscious only opens itself to these areas if we are completely relaxed; we must release all tension throughout our body, whether in sitting or lying down, and then breathing deeply, look at the situation or the person with whom we are in conflict. Without objectifying or reflecting and analyzing, we seek to become one, to commune with that which we are looking at while blessing calmly without attempting to feel anything.

The effects of this forgiveness in depth are stupendous! It is Christ Himself who saves and re-creates us. Th e first beneficiary of forgiveness is the one who practices it. Deep knots, which also have their physical expression in the body, are untied and an unexpected freedom enters into our whole being, opening the channels of divine life and allowing a new attitude into our existence. All who are familiar with this commandment of Christ and practice it know its miracles, not only in the liberation of self, but in the turning around of situations or in the seemingly impossible transformation of another person.

The practice of this work on oneself will progressively reveal that we have many more enemies than we thought! Beyond all the traumas of our undigested past, beginning with our parents whom we find so difficult to forgive for giving us life, and through them God Himself for the same reason, we also fi nd it hard to forgive ourselves, for we cannot accept ourselves as we are. I am my first neighbor and I must look at myself as God looks at me! It all begins with this effort. If we see enemies on the outside, it is because they live within us! Thus every relationship can be rotten because we project the face of our father on the one of a friend or of a stranger. A situation can be polluted because it makes us relive something from our distant past. In a way, everything that makes us react is an enemy, everything and everyone that we judge are enemies, and finally everything that bothers us! That is why the Desert Fathers could say that a day without vexation is a lost day, because it is in the love of enemies that is found the unique characteristic of Christianity, its newness and its essence; it is in the love of enemies that the ego is crucified and that an unhoped-for life becomes possible: the very experience of the resurrected Christ.

6 Sloth

The person who advances on the path and responds to the call of God passes through the successive stages of an indispensable purification. After the enthusiastic departure, oft en lived in euphoria and in a courageous battle, comes, as with the Hebrew people, the stage of the desert and maturation. In this great dryness, this mysterious crisis, we begin to complain in regard to everything and to think nostalgically of "Egypt," of former pleasures. We no longer have any desire for the spiritual life. God, if He exists, seems absent or distant and all that we do appears completely useless.

This is not a longing or an impulse as it is with the other passions, but a state which seizes and penetrates all the levels of the soul, paralyzes our conscience and, as Maximus the Confessor says,

167

gives free rein to all the other passions. John Cassian adds that this stage has two characteristics: disgust and fear which infiltrate all our actions. From them is born an interior bad mood which makes the moment unbearable. We question everything, not only God, but the monastic life, marriage, the path and its crosses. We can sink into the most hellish desperation and suicidal depression. Images of another life come to us: life would be better in other places and circumstances than those which we have. The monk dreams of leaving his monastery to become a bishop, married couples look at other men and women, or escape into the children, sleep, work, alcohol. Each one finds his escape, but in all cases, it is a sleep of the spirit. According to Maximus the Confessor, sloth is the final product of a person lost in desire, sadness, and anger. It crushes us with the horrible distress of the meaninglessness and absurdity of our life. That is our greatest fear in the twentieth century, far beyond nuclear danger: the meaninglessness of life.

Because this crisis most often arises in the middle of life, around age forty, the Fathers have called it "the demon of noon"; but we can be "forty years old" at twenty or sixty, depending on the maturity of our spiritual growth. And this demon can appear under a shining sun or on a gray rainy day when, without any reason, weariness suddenly takes hold of us.

The worst enemy, then, and certainly in an unconscious way, is the person who seeks to console us! Consolation is the last remedy, not only because it merely increases the pain, but because it also inhibits the process of conversion. The person who is affected by sloth can do only one thing — live fully and consciously that which is given him to live: disgust, fear, weariness, bad moods, depression. To be that, to really live one's disgust and fear in prayer and surrender, is the loving "yes" to God who manifests Himself in the face of the present moment. It is our Creator who chooses to come to us as He wishes and He knows the reasons why. As a Father, He gives us in each moment that which is best for us, even if the limits of our intelligence keep us from understanding this. We must let ourselves be led into the unfulfillment of our subconscious in order to be fulfilled; the one who does not descend into the darkness does not desire the light: "I must descend into my hell to cry toward heaven," said St. John of Kronstadt.

The desert is, therefore, one of the greatest mysteries on the way. It puts us at the foot of the wall: according to our decision, it leads to the hardening of the heart with all the tragedies listed above, or to the entry into the promised land, even if the "milk and honey" do not yet flow. The hour of our greatest freedom has rung, a turning point is at hand which, quite often, provides a specific direction for the rest of our life, especially when this is a crisis of the "forties." We cast off our ego and progressively cut all our anchors in order to place all our cares on God alone and finally enter into endless wisdom; or, on the contrary, we fall into temptation and give ourselves over to the madness of the world.

In sloth, we must remember that life is like a line made up of many points: we are never asked to live more than one point at a time, here and now, in the present moment. "Let the day's own trouble be sufficient for the day" (Mt. 6:34). When St. Thérèse of Lisieux could no longer bear her suffering, she said that she lived everything through love "from moment to moment."

7 Vanity

The feeling of "look at me," according to all patristic literature, accompanies spiritual progress like a shadow. This is an internal reaction, almost uncontrollable for it escapes the influence of our will, as John Cassian observed. It can put on many aspects and intrude into everything, even into our good actions. This is a neurotic need to be recognized and to give oneself importance in order to live. The ego always wants to be the center of things, at every moment. It values its appearance, its voice, its origin, its qualities, its beauty, its knowledge. Often it is disappointed or upset that others have not noticed it! A vain person loves to be looked at and enjoys seeing how others honor him. He makes of life a theater on which he is center stage and his self wears the masks of his roles. In doing this, say the Fathers, he truncates the goal of life: his ego takes the place of God. But his armor is very fragile. The more his past is inhabited with frustrations and his present with insecurity, the more he is susceptible and irritable, always on the lookout for admiration or disparagement.

The immediate consequence is the destruction of outgoingness through hatred, jealousy and arrogance.

In the face of this insecurity of the present, the vain person fills his future with illusions. This is the second aspect of his evil. He sees himself becoming a great saint around whom others gather. There again the theatrics continue, concrete reality is lost sight of, the present is smoke-filled, and he does not truly incarnate himself. Saint John Climacus calls him a coward, for his life is not involvement, but a game. To concentrate on that which is "uniquely necessary" becomes impossible, prayer is hypocritical and without consistency, virtues are travesties. The scale on which the vain person can play is without limits: from the feeling of "look at me" which constantly accompanies every action, to the demonic monster we call pride.

The great remedy for vanity is to fix our gaze upon Christ rather than upon ourselves: "It is not I who lives, but Christ who lives in me" (Gal. 2:20), not the egocentric but the Christocentric "I." That is the very goal of the Jesus Prayer! But perhaps it is even more fruitful to let oneself be looked at by Christ, by His gaze of infinite love which never leaves us. From this, we can slowly learn that everything contains this gaze and this love, since everything without exception is a gift of God. Nothing is owed us, everything at each moment is offered to us by Him: "What have you that you did not receive?" (1 Cor. 4:7). This consciousness which the Jesus Prayer makes possible, which places the holy name on all that comes near to us, calls forth praise and thanksgiving, frees us from the constraining need for ownership, and especially liberates the "inner man." We feel ourselves recognized by God and marvel at being so fulfilled that we have no more need of external support.

8 Pride

If vanity is like a shadow which follows us everywhere, pride is its fulfillment in darkness. What has been said of vanity goes for pride as well, except that it is not satisfied with illusions and takes action, making lies its most concrete reality. Saint John Climacus defines it as betrayal of God and destruction of the person. For other Fathers, pride is blasphemy, the sin of Satan. According to Evagrius, it falls upon those who have advanced on the spiritual journey, and leads them to believe that they are the authors of their progress or of their virtues. Pride lives as though God did not exist. It lives through itself, without God, and considers that it is the exclusive source of its being and activity. It puts itself in God's place and gives itself His attributes! This is what Lucifer did and which he continually proposes to human beings from the beginning. This darkness of the spirit has a double characteristic: it does not recognize the fundamental incapacity of humanity after the fall, nor that God is the Creator of all that exists, the source of all good. Through the wound that he brings to love, states Maximus the Confessor, the person of pride crucifies Christ anew. Living outside of himself, he also puts God outside and anyone else who threatens his ego: to not be recognized or, worse yet, to be criticized, can throw him into furor or bitterness. Those are the best tests to prove that "he has no roots in himself " (Mt. 13:20) and that he has lost the peaceful kernel of his being.

 The only antidote for pride, which is the source of all evil, is humility, the source of all good and the foundation of the Prayer of the Heart. There is no room for God in an obstructed heart, and that is why the goal of the ascetic is to break pride and to make of humility his new foundation. But the humble person is not weak or groveling. On the contrary, he has found his axis in God. Freed from himself and from the weight of his ego, he is in his right place, aligned with his being. Such a person has become " humility," that is to say, humus, or fertile soil.

Look at this earth: it offers itself to the farmer, becomes receptive and meek, opens itself to the seed as to a promise, carries it in its depths in gestation, and permits this life deposited within it to fulfill itself in plenitude. The humble person is this earth which receives the name of Jesus in surrender and absolute confidence; he gives himself completely to this work which is beyond him but which nevertheless would not be accomplished without his collaboration. This is an alliance of love, the union of divine and human wills where the least self- love is a rupture and a betrayal. It is on this major obstacle that asceticism works. But in order that it not fall into the inevitable will to power and possession, a pride more subtle and satanic than any other, it must have humility as its foundation.

The Jesus Prayer beseeches humility like a grace to be received, and inscribes immediately in this attitude: "Have pity upon me, a sinner!" This is nothing other than the most radical love which, in naming Jesus, empties itself of self and enters into the annihilation of the Master, "who, though He was in the form of God, humbled Himself and became obedient unto death, even death on the cross" (Phil 2:6). God reveals in Jesus the depth of love and in naming Himself shows us the features of our possible resemblance to Him.

For God alone is humble, and "we cannot describe the power nor the essence of this sun which is humility" (St. John Climacus), except in receiving its radiance. When God descends into the human heart through prayer, He mysteriously reveals what is in His own heart. And in this incredible intimacy between God and human beings, we can guess something of the intimacy at the heart of the three divine Persons, where one gives itself in fullness to the other. Each of the three Persons is itself only in giving itself to the other two, each being itself only by being out of itself, in the total abnegation of self which is at the same time a movement toward the Other. This is ecstasy toward "You," infinite and pure Love without the shadow of folding back upon itself. When God descends toward us, it is in this same movement of limitless self-giving, "obedient unto death on the cross." Jesus Christ never ceases to descend into the depths of our human condition, in the thickness of our flesh, in our suff ering and death, in our hell, in our daily bread and finally in our heart, seeking

in an intimate face-to-face in order to say what is said from all
eternity in God: "You!" And, having done this, He effaces Himself
completely by blending into our blood, our flesh, our breath.

It is always in this process of "annihilation" that God is God; that
is, that He reveals His being, His name: "Therefore God has highly
exalted Him and bestowed on Him the name which is above every
name" (Phil. 2:9). This attitude places surrender at the root of true
being. It is only in entering into this attitude that we discover our
own being and the holy name which rests there as an incandescent
cone. For love is reciprocity, annihilation for the other. Our heart will
open only through the departure of the little self and of all the
demons that have produced it. In this self-emptying, our identity is
unveiled on the way to resemblance with its God whose glory is
revealed on the cross — love offered to the end. There, at the
intersection of the descent of one toward the other, is found the
encounter which the Jesus Prayer calls upon and recognizes at the
moment of its realization: "When God sees that, in purity of heart,
you trust Him more than yourself, then an unknown power will come
into you and make its home there. And you will feel in all your senses
the power of the One who is with you" (St. Isaac the Syrian).
Humility is God Himself.

It is only on this backdrop that we can understand the oft en terrible
asceticism of the saints and their message often so abrupt; this is
simply the imitation of Christ giving Himself for them. Therefore,

the sentence which is heard most oft en from the great masters of monasticism is: "The beginning of salvation is the condemnation of oneself." The greater repentance is, the more the path is shortened, repeat ceaselessly all the spiritual teachers through our twenty centuries of history. Abba Poemen summarized the teaching of the tradition of the ancients in this phrase: "To weep is the traditional way taught by Scripture and by the Fathers, who tell us: weep, for there is no other way than this one."

What else can we do faced with the overwhelming humbling of Christ and our prideful behavior, our indifference, and our cowardice? Submerged in bitterness and despair, torn by so much hatred and destruction, standing before love which, nevertheless, opens its arms on the cross, we must let the tears fl ow. The heart is wounded and it is through this wound that the intellect can descend and liberate the divine energy of the prayer which then leads to great progress. Tears are the sign that, already, grace has penetrated us and that our heart is breaking; the affections are seized, so transformation becomes possible. The heart is no longer a stone and opens to new life under the tears which are a baptismal fountain. Throughout our life, this baptism becomes more interior until the day when repentance will break down the doors of our depths: "Have pity upon me, a sinner!" The tears spring forth, the heart becomes a womb where these waters purify and regenerate it, making it a place for rebirth in Christ.

This humiliation, a descent into the depths of our interior baptistry, fi rst configures us to the agony of Jesus and to His death. With Him, we live our own death; like Him, we abandon ourselves willingly to it, and this act calls forth an attitude profoundly linked to the Jesus Prayer: the constant memory of death. "May the memory of death be present when you go to sleep and when you awaken, along with the invocation of Jesus" (St. John Climacus). Th ere is evidently nothing more radical against the passions, which explains the unanimity of the Fathers around this supreme remedy. To live one's death here and now, to really accept it and even choose it in a "yes" which becomes more and more real, takes away its sting; for Christ, whose name we never cease to pronounce, can then descend into this opening that we offer Him, and through His death vanquish our death.

The person who does not live every day with his death does not live at all, and does not know the fullness of life! This is where we experience how such humility is the foundation of the life. "Th e constant memory of death," says Hesychius, "determines the exclusion of all vain worry, the watch of the spirit and constant prayer, detachment from the body, hatred of sin. All virtue is born from this remembering. Let us practice this remembrance in the same way that we breathe." Isaac the Syrian adds that the love of God leads the soul to life and fills the heart, bringing us toward "the deep contemplation of which it is not possible to speak." This view of the apex of life is a far cry from the horrifying emptiness which awaits everyone at the end of their days as a final and fatal catastrophe. Christ has transformed death into the great initiator of life; the Jesus Prayer plunges us into the Paschal mystery of our Lord where we become participants in His victory.

One of the great levers in our collaboration appears when our prayer is accompanied by the feeling of being nothing. If we exercise this attitude until "we feel our nothingness from the bottom of the heart, then the Lord will always be there, He who creates and has created all things from nothing" (Theophan the Recluse). The greatness of our suffering will be in relation to our passions, and the pain can be intense and make us taste the dereliction of Golgotha, but it is lived in a peaceful certainty which senses and heralds the resurrection. "What happiness," says Origen, "to admit that we are miserable, for God grants me a Liberator." This is also the word of St. Paul: "When I am weak, then I am strong" (2 Cor. 2:10), and St. Thérèse of Lisieux: "My secret is to always remain small … How happy I am since I no longer seek to satisfy myself!" It is an amazing joy to be nothing, an unexpected liberation in which we find ourselves projected, as though the chains of our hell were broken and the tombstone of our heart lifted!

To live with death is to live as a resurrected one. We must rejoice at being nothing! Then the power of the resurrected Lord is at work within us. And on the way, beneath the baptism of tears, arises the smile of new life: "He who is on the way with interior tears according to God never ceases to celebrate … and knows the spiritual smile of the soul" (St. John Climacus).

This joy is the characteristic of the one who has reached the other side, a joy unconnected to any external condition, always there because it is the very presence of the Holy Spirit. This joy is truly vital for prayer because "the prayer of the sad man does not have the strength to rise to the altar of God" (Hermas). It is, therefore, of the highest importance to always place ourselves in this right tonality of joy, to harmonize ourselves with the presence of the Spirit which is joy within us. Many Christians ignore the fact that this is a commandment which runs throughout the New Testament and is its substance: "Rejoice in the Lord always; again I will say, Rejoice!" (Phil. 4:4).

Where else could we better exercise obedience and renunciation of our own will? Asceticism surely reaches here its ultimate goal, when the mystery of Easter truly becomes an "instrument" to live here and now. There is not a single vexation in our daily life that cannot be transformed by it. To be giving thanks "in all times and places" no matter what happens because God is at work — what death to self, but what life! The Jesus Prayer permits us to place the holy name on every event at each moment and to decipher the real meaning of history. When difficulties are transformed in this way, by the sweat of our brow, there are no more enemies! The love of our enemies is the greatest humility and the criterion of all progress. "I

share everything with Christ, both the Spirit and the body, the nails and the Resurrection"
(St. Gregory of Nazianzus). Indeed, what the prayer entreats us first of all is to keep the commandments that are nothing other than the description of Christ and His beauty, which we slowly let ourselves be entrusted with through this incessant prayer.

9 Watchfulness

External solitude and silence can be, and have been, useful conditions for hesychia, but they can also be, for those who are not guided, paths of loss of reason, of endless interior chatter, in which a thousand demons assail the feelings and thoughts. It is written that "there where your treasure is, so also is your heart," and as long as the heart is not the throne of God, it is at the mercy of infernal powers and lets escape thoughts, images and feelings that are out of control. To free oneself from all thoughts and worries presupposes a continual interior battle, the "invisible warfare," whose ultimate weapon is *nepsis*, that is, the state of restraint, of extreme vigilance or attention.

All of these terms are inseparable and quasi-synonymous among the Fathers. Only the restraint of thoughts and worries makes possible union with God and contemplative knowledge, for it releases us from our troubles and our passions, and gives us, with the help of grace, a pure heart. Hesychius the Sinaite even identifies *nepsis* with the pure heart and makes it the pivotal point of all his teaching, the way which "procures all the goods of the century to come and the fullness of virtues which lead to true prayer."

Saint Peter taught, and the Church reminds us of it every day: "Be sober, be watchful. Your adversary the devil prowls around like a roaring lion, seeking someone to devour" (1 Pet. 5:8). As skilled experts of the human soul and of psychoanalysis, the Fathers discerned the stages of demonic temptation:

-- It begins innocently by a simple *suggestion*, some word or picture without sin.
-- If the soul *dialogues* with it, then comes the assent which is already guilty and which can slip into passion when "the object lodges for a long time in the soul and it gets used to it" (St. John Climacus).
-- Finally comes the *captivity*, where the heart is dragged along involuntarily, the object having become its "treasure."

It is in this context that is found nepsis, as a watchman on the lookout, watching for the subtlest surprise from the Adversary, filtering every thought which presents itself and crushing it before it can begin to grow and gain strength. To enter into dialogue with a temptation is to lose the battle. This is the price of the watch of the heart, and the tradition of the ascetics unanimously seeks to pay it. Saint Basil says that we must "watch over ourselves and always have our attention in an awakened state."

181

In the west, St. Gregory the Great said of St. Benedict: "I can say of this real man that he lived with himself since he was always attentive to watch over himself, holding himself constantly in the Presence of his Creator, examining himself endlessly, never letting his watch over his soul be distracted." And St. Gregory added: "Each time a dangerous preoccupation drags us out of ourselves, we remain ourselves and yet we are no longer with ourselves: we lose sight of ourselves and are diffused in external things."

"To enter into oneself," as the prodigal son did after having lived outside in the company of pigs (Lk. 15), is to maintain an intense consciousness of ourselves which is radically different from the ordinary attitude of forgetfulness in which we constantly let ourselves get carried away. We must become keenly conscious in the present moment. Abba Isaiah states: "Do not do or say anything without having examined it and scrutinized the intention which motivates you; and do all this in the presence of God." Our greatness and decadence are at stake in that moment of freedom between suggestion and assent. This is a critical crossroad which originates all holiness and all separation. Considering our fragility and the slyness of the demon who can drape itself with light in order to lie to us, it is best to cut short every suggestion. In doing so, we root out sin at its source and in its very principle. Though it must be held in check, sin is merely the negative aspect of this battle of the attention whose goal is "the quest for prayer." Perpetual prayer is the great means for awakening and sustaining our attention.

Attention, vigilance, consciousness of self or presence to self and God are all synonymous. They are the very core of the spiritual life, a way which, according to the ancients, "leads to all virtues and to all God's commandments in the Old and New Testaments. Watchfulness completely liberates us from passionate thoughts and words and from bad actions, if we persevere. It gives a sure knowledge of God and opens the divine and hidden mysteries. This is truly purity of heart and gives us access to contemplation" (Hesychius of Bates).

Vigilance is progressively bought at a great price through prayer and asceticism. Wherever we are, whatever we are doing and without necessarily stopping our work, we must become conscious of ourselves and of God. This requires relaxation, especially in the neck and the shoulders, the chest and the stomach, and an entrance with one's whole body into an attitude of trust and surrender to what is here and now; our breathing becomes deeper in the diaphragm, our center of gravity being in the middle and not in the head. The Jesus Prayer can then sometimes be said in all truth, inscribing itself in our being and in the situation which is occupying our attention.

In the beginning, this requires some effort, but later it becomes spontaneous, as though second nature. Already at the end of several weeks, the fruits of this practice will manifest themselves in a surprising way. For the bell of the monastery, which rings every hour as a "reminder" for the monk, can be substituted by the "bip-bip" of the quartz watch on the wrist of the layperson, to "remind" him every hour in his interior cell! These are real holes of light in this world of darkness, an oasis in the desert. Little by little, the whole day can radiate with this new presence, as though the hours were getting closer to each other. Our reasons to live modify themselves and under the daily weight of routine is revealed a supreme joy. Appearances become transparence.

Someday, the Jesus Prayer will no longer leave us if this battle is fought with courage and perseverance. It will be as intimate and inseparable to us as our breath itself, and everything will be interconnected: the interior and the exterior, the visible and the invisible. As the coming and going of the breath which carries it, the holy name placed on all that surrounds it "breathes into everything a divine breath" (Gen. 2:7) and we can live in all truth, experiencing the infinite in the finite of things and eternity in passing time. Instead of living on the surface, we "let down our nets into the deep" (Lk. 5:4) as Christ invites us to do.

These "reminders" create in the one who practices them an entirely different atmosphere, thanks to energies which they put to work and which truly regenerate us. Through vigilance in its pure state, the "pure heart," there are no more thoughts, images, or feelings, but only Being. To simply be conscious of that which IS, without judging or reacting is to commune with the One who IS and who reveals to us His name as He did to Moses at the burning bush: "I am the One Who is." This is the depth of all that exists and that we encounter, as long as we do not interpose a mental screen between us and the experience. The Jesus Prayer frees us from all other suggestion from the mental and "reminds" us of the evidence: "You will die in your sins unless you believe that I am He," said Christ (Jn. 8:24).

The name and the way are, therefore, one and the same! "Believe that I am" is to adhere to that which is here and now; the opposite is separation, that is to say, sin, and therefore death. The Buddha also announced this: "Vigilance is the way of immortality; inattention, the way of death." Patanjali (the father of yoga, fourth century bc) said: "The practice is the intensity of permanent vigilance." It is interesting to know that all the religious traditions are unanimous on this teaching and agree that almost nothing happens as long as we have not taken vigilance as the great means of asceticism.

The adventure of the Apostles on the Sea of Galilee reveals this clearly (Matt. 14:22): to live without Christ or to take Him for a "ghost" is to be in the night and the storm, "troubled with fear," disoriented. But the gaze fixed on Him allows us to master our daily life. All lack of watchfulness swallows us up in the waters of events and only the prayer allows us to grasp anew the extended hand of Jesus.

This is the goal: to live with our sights fixed on Christ. In order not to be distracted (pulled out of oneself) by daily life, we must lean upon Him, as St. Peter did on the water; that is, live consciously each moment and adhere to it, carried by the call of Christ: "Lord Jesus Christ, Son of God, have mercy on me, a sinner." The consciousness of self and of that which surrounds us are then made one. There is no more external and we take on the habit of "looking outside as though we were looking within." Everything in us is reception, non-objectification, absence of desire, pure and simple vision, non-judgment and communion.

This attitude of watchfulness is a complete stranger to the ego which disappears before it. The ego is always active on the surface while watchfulness is a "non-action," an encounter in depth, in the silence of being from which we receive everything and which leads us at every step. We then live in an absolute freedom from result and yet in an extraordinary fruitfulness. We become inhabited by the very consciousness of Christ. To be conscious of Him in all the levels of our being, to be possessed by Him and to possess Him in ourselves and in all things, to taste His presence in all experiences whether passive or active, this is the crowning of personal consciousness and the summit of all joy.

But it is also the summit of asceticism to wish to be entirely and exclusively consecrated to this new consciousness. Every obstacle must be removed, even that which seems good. To be on the way with a divided will, a small fraction of our energy and a mental hesitation, leads nowhere! We must break radically with our habits, with our way of being and introduce into ourselves — through a decisive act which shakes our whole nature — a new idea-force, a consecration of our energies to Jesus Christ so complete that to live from Him becomes for our heart the only desire, and for our will the only activity in all that we live and do. From then on, all other desires and needs enter into a process of conversion and concentrate in a unique passion for Christ. This is not an intellectual concentration, but a physical, psychic and spiritual consciousness in which everything is felt, seen, and wanted in the Lord. We must make of each detail, each form of life, each incident and movement a nourishment filled with the holy name in order to feed the divine fire which inhabits us. As long as we still live and act for egotistic motives, we remain slaves of an inferior consciousness: we do not act for God but for our personal satisfaction and the consent of our inclinations.

The Lord will not manifest Himself as long as we are in search of ourselves. Our whole way of being, all our actions, even the insignificant ones, can and must be lived as sacred acts in a consciousness offering to God. Everything must be directed toward Him; nothing must be undertaken for ourselves or for other interests. Only then will the supports of the ego, its presence and influence, its last refuge, be eliminated and all life become a single adoration.

Behind everything, there is the presence: we must feel it always and everywhere, awaken to its constant, intimate, enveloping nearness, intensely perceive it and commune with it in every moment.

To turn all our emotions toward this presence of Christ is the most intense way of purification for the heart. Sooner or later "the pure in heart will see God," will feel Him, touch Him, hear Him, smell Him. All the senses, members and vital functions will be invested with this divine light-force which moves, feels and thinks in us (Acts 1:8). We will be submerged in God. We can be and will be one day as was St. Seraphim of Sarov, a true sun of light. In a way we already are at the very beginning of the journey, in the most humble contact with this same light which is also within us, the same light which inhabits the greatest of saints.

In the beginning, we perceive it as a small vibration of silence in the background of our being; we discover eventually that it is always there as a depth behind our consciousness and that we can rest in it at will even in the midst of the daily whirlwind. But progressively it becomes more and more clear, like an immense silent ocean which vibrates in our depths, a real presence with which the Jesus Prayer links up, dialogues with, pulls living waters as from a well.

As we move forward, the prayer settling in more permanently, the intellect becomes still, and we discover that we no longer need to think in order to act or speak or do something. With the habit of referring constantly to the presence within us, everything is given us at the moment it is wished for: without any reflection, the right word springs forth and everything without exception comes without eff ort through the silence of thought and will, the complete subsiding in the One who can do everything. This is another way of life, the one of the Gospel. Here action truly becomes contemplation. Whether we eat, work, or go for a walk, we remain connected and let the same power run through everything. This power is consciousness, source of life. Nothing troubles it, no thoughts, images or events, even violent ones, can affect this interior peace.

Our humanity is the crossroad of the finite and the infi nite, and the incessant prayer awakens and develops our consciousness of this reality. Behind the Jesus Prayer is found His Presence, His Consciousness of which our consciousness is the reflection just as the moon reflects the sun. For there to be a "full" moon, it must expose itself fully, be completely receptive and receive the infusion of solar light to the point of absorbing it in its depths and become itself the light. This is the becoming of our consciousness in reciprocity with the divine consciousness. In asceticism, it is not a matter of "fighting against," but of transmuting everything while never losing contact with the divine sun.

"This consciousness," said Theophan the Recluse, "is the most powerful lever which exists in the mechanism of the spiritual life."

Chapter Six
THE MEANING OF THE PRAYER

Lord Jesus Christ, Son of God,
have mercy on me, a sinner.

Why this prayer and not another one? Why these words and not others? Because this is the true language, the complete language, "full of grace and truth," subject-verb-divine complements, such as were transmitted to us through tradition by our Mother-Church, in order to live as true disciples.

Like every mother does for her child, the Church first spelled out the words during the early centuries until we entered into the fullness of language. It was a tender stammering at first. But having finally reached wisdom, we could no longer speak like the ignorant: "When I was a child, I spoke like a child; when I became a man, I gave up childish ways" (1 Cor. 13:11). Even when the child can say only one word, "bread," for instance, he wants to express: "I would like a piece of bread." Thus in the early days of the Church, when only one prayer was pronounced, such as the name "Jesus" alone, or "Lord, save me" and many other short formulas, they were already inhabited by the entire phrase and the fullness of faith which it confesses: "Lord Jesus Christ, have mercy on me, a sinner." The intelligence and the heart were nourished by the right confession, and entire generations gave their lives for it in the earliest days of the faith.

Today everything is complicated. Mircea Eliade observed that two thousand years of history is enough for religion to fossilize. In aging, we risk falling back into childhood, but without its grace. We have lost the incredible freshness of the Acts of the Apostles, where we can still see the true tonality of the Christian. The nourishing link with founding centuries and the great tradition is broken. Like disoriented and amnesiac old folks, we are "tossed to and fro and carried about with every wind of doctrine, by the cunning of men" (Eph. 4:14); "For a time is coming when people will not endure sound teaching, but having itching ears they will accumulate for themselves teachers to suit their own liking, and will turn away from listening to the truth and wander into myths" (2 Tim. 4:3). Saint Paul could not have made a better diagnosis of Christianity in its state of decay nor of contemporary people, who, having become "strangers to themselves," are given over to the prodigious delirium of our industrialized world.

Where is the word to be found which gives structure to an adult Christian, and the Spirit which introduces us into the transforming experience? Some suggest that a person who repeats "Jesus" — "Jesus," in some sentimental subjectivity risks a terrible fall. But let us not throw out too quickly the way followed by the spiritual giants of the Sinai. When we have years of asceticism and prayer behind us, of humble submission to the tradition, it is possible that the Spirit "which fills everything" will indeed have us repeat a single word. It will then moan within us the rising up of divine mystery in its fullness, and not God à la carte according to our pious fantasies.

For those who seriously wish to take up the way, Anthony Bloom states that "the doctrinal and spiritual wealth of the Jesus Prayer is infinite; it is not only the summary but the whole of faith whose enigma Christ resolves." Here is the word and the Spirit opening our depths to the depths of God (Eph. 3:14–19). The Jesus Prayer, in its complete expression, puts to work the whole person, body- soul- spirit, revealing to him the complete God three times blessed, Father- Son- Spirit. This is a synergy in which "God becomes man so that man might become god" (St. Athanasius). The Jesus Prayer reveals to us God's design for humanity, and at the same time makes us experience the One in whom is first realized the design: Jesus Christ.

Through His life in history and in us, Jesus reveals to each person the ways of God. Each word of the prayer is a "fullness" in itself, irreplaceable, offering something of His celestial and hidden energy, already partly lived by the tradition and revealing itself more and more as we progress on the way. This is the meaning of the mysterious future contained in the revelation of the holy name to Moses, which we can translate in this way: "You will know that I AM when you will have experienced what I will do for you" (Ex. 3:12, defined in 33:16). The revelation of the name makes itself dependent on our attention to the present: it is in the heart of the present moment that is revealed the Absolute Present "I AM" of which the prayer is the unending unveiling.

But in order to nourish it and allow it to become a real sacrament, it is vital to take our time and to place ourselves before each word separately for long moments. All the ancients whom we have met insisted on the importance of this effort. No one can say, unless it is through personal experience, what the Spirit wants to teach us (Jn. 14:26 and 16:13). Whoever has not let himself be ploughed, sowed for three to six hours in a day, does not know that it is the "voice of the Dove" which is muffled in his depths (Song 2:12). To stay there, in silence and without reflection, with all other voices still: "If you continue in My word, you are truly My disciples, and you will know the truth, and the truth will set you free" (Jn. 8:31); to remain for a long time in a single word, then the next, and finally in the entire prayer — that is when it will bear many fruits and "if My words abide in you, ask whatever you will, and it shall be done for you" (Jn. 15:7).

This union, as intimate and fertile as that of the vine and its branches, forged by the word, takes root and leans constantly upon the objective givens of the tradition to receive their verification and criteria. Here are several major points to begin our personal meditation.

1. " Lord"

In this slow gestation, we discover from the first word that the Jesus Prayer cannot be the product of our fantasies, but only, as for Mary who is the archetype of the way, the blessed fruit of our depths fertilized by the Holy Spirit. "Jesus is Lord" is a revelation, not a human concept (Rom. 10:9). It is the name which reveals perfectly the mystery of Christ, Son of man, issued from humanity, and Son of God, issued from God. The joining of the two happens within us when, visited by the grace of the Spirit of God, our human lips, our intelligence and our heart are able to say of Jesus that He is "Lord." Indeed, "no one can say 'Jesus is Lord' except by the Holy Spirit" (1 Cor. 12:3). It is, therefore, much more than an expression or some sort of prayer: the Jesus Prayer is an act which is both prophetic and political. "Prophetic" because in saying "Lord" we are inspired as were the prophets by the Holy Spirit, and "political" because we enter into a radically new reading of history. These two dimensions live in us, and when we enter into the Lordship of Jesus, we become sons with Him through grace.

In this sense, the Jesus Prayer is an act, but the word "Lord" is its preamble without which we cannot enter further. Before penetrating into the Holy of Holies which is the name of Jesus, we must take our shoes off, as Moses did before the burning bush, and bypass the little self (Ex. 3:3–5).

This is above all a unique and privileged relationship! If Jesus is Lord, nothing lives outside of Him and all things, without exception, are in Him (Col. 1:16–17). If He is truly "Lord" for me, I accept in turn to enter with Him into an absolute and unconditional dependence. I receive myself from Him in every moment like the air that I breathe, and I can do nothing of myself or under other impulses without betraying Him. He is God, source of my life, and my life is His kingdom whereas Lord He has all rights. Nothing in me, therefore, is unknown to Him, everything in me is "from Him, by Him and in Him."

All the inclinations of the heart and the authenticity of our prayer is screened and verified here. How many other lords have we in our life? Where are our secret preferences, what nourishes and vivifies us? "There where your treasure is, so also is your heart!" (Mt. 6:21) — this is a statement which may be cruel but necessary to bring us out of our illusions if Jesus is not the Lord of our life.

Everything begins with this test where, as with Abraham, we will discover what our Isaac is "that we hold dear," so that we may off er it to God and become free from all other dependence (Gen. 22:1–19). Abraham truly died the day of "his" sacrifice, but it is also on that day that he came to life and became "the Father of all believers."

To say of Jesus that He is "Lord" is a death for us. We must die to all that is not Him and which improperly occupies His place in our hearts. The first Christians, who are our norm, did not hesitate as worthy "sons of Abraham" to go all the way. The word " Lord" was reserved only for Yahweh by the Jews, and for the emperor by the Romans. To place it upon someone else was to be condemned to death. Thus began three centuries of martyrdom. All who asked for baptism in the name of Jesus and recognized Him as Lord were persecuted. They accepted, and happily moreover, to suffer and die for Him. These are our foundations, those of the Church and those of each Christian in particular. The act which opens the Jesus Prayer is normative throughout the centuries: it is a decision which culminates in the baptism of blood. I know today that, in saying to Jesus "Lord" I will die for Him. "I die every day," says St. Paul, because "for me to live is Christ" (1 Cor. 15:31 and Phil. 1:21).

It is a decision of life or death which is at the foundation of the act of the prayer and which gives it its style. We enter into it without reserve in an immense humility, without the shadow of triumphalism or the pride of knowledge. Our whole being prostrates itself internally before the holy name, with tenderness and adoration, but also with that sacred trembling which the Jews had when pronouncing the awesome name of Yahweh.

This humility is all the greater because it will make it possible for the "Lord" to act with power and to shake the empire of all the false gods within and around us. To deny that the emperor was "Lord" was a political act. It is the same today as well, and perhaps even more so: at the heart of a consumer society, we affirm that nothing and no one outside of the Lord Jesus can satisfy our hunger which is a hunger for God. From this perspective, all politics which do not seek their purpose in the spiritual dimension are opium for the people. One of the most phenomenal acts that Jesus as "Lord" placed in history was the washing of His disciples' feet. "You call Me Teacher and Lord; and you are right, for so I am. If I then, your Lord and Teacher, have washed your feet, you also ought to wash one another's feet" (Jn. 13:13–14). The Lordship of Jesus becomes an axe at the root of all systems and all authority, of all established orders or disorders, as well as in all individual existence which does not get on its knees before humanity to serve it (Mt. 25:31–46).

2. " Jesus"

Jesus, therefore, stands in history and opens it to its self-transcendence. Since the coming of Jesus, history is a temple of his mysterious presence; it is only as such that it finds its meaning and finally becomes History, fulfilling itself in Him, the "Liberator of the world." This is the etymological content of the word "Jesus"

itself, which means " Savior," "Liberation," "Salvation." The
prophets announced Him as the One who would take upon Himself
all our pain, for in Him "God is with us," Emmanuel (Ish. 53 and
7:14; Mt. 1:23). And that is why it is the "Name which is above every
name, that at the name of Jesus every knee should bow, in heaven
and on earth and under the earth" (Phil. 2:9–11).

At Christmas, God enters into history through a man named Jesus,
in a specific time two thousand years ago, and in a particular country,
Bethlehem in Judea. From the time of the Ascension and Pentecost,
God is present through this same Jesus in all of history, in the hearts
of all people, in all times and in all countries: "I am the Alpha and
the Omega, the first and the last, the beginning and the end" (Rev.
22:13). In naming Him, we find ourselves in the incandescent point
of all that exists and of all transformation through Jesus, our center
and the center of the universe. But to attain to Jesus means fi rst to
hear this question: "Who do you say that I am?" (Mt. 16:15). And our
life which stammers a response is always sent back to the Gospel
where the Jesus of history reveals to us the ways of God. "Learn
from Me," He tells us (Mt. 11:29). To know Him through a long
familiarity with the Gospel allows us to recognize Him within us, in
the face-to-face intimacy which no other teaching can replace. Only
personal experience will tell us who Jesus really is. If this knowledge
becomes the supreme interest of our life, beyond our problems and
even our sins, the beauty of Jesus will seize us completely and will be
the secret of our metamorphosis.

To know Him is then to be reborn anew toward unknown levels of consciousness, to be healed of all our evil, even while remaining sick with the stigmatas of the fall; it is also to escape all the spirits under heaven, to be pulled away from dangers and death. There is no problem or worry which does not find its answer in Him: Jesus does not save us once and for all, but in every moment. We are never alone, and everything can find transparence and light in Him. That is where, in the heart of human beings, the transformation of the world begins. The social is a dimension of the personal: the other becomes brother or sister and sacrament of the divine presence if our prayer is not mere pious smoke.

But if it is true that no one can say that Jesus is Lord without the Holy Spirit, no one can recognize Him without Him, and we only learn the ways of God through the action within us of Jesus and of the Spirit. To say "Jesus" in the prayer is to receive, as He did, the unction of the Spirit which descends with power upon us in order to guide us into all truth (Jn. 16:13). The Spirit teaches us about Jesus because Jesus is the Christ, the holy One anointed by the Spirit (Acts 10:38).

3. " Jesus Christ"

After thirty years of silence, when Jesus spoke
for the first time in public while "all eyes were upon him" full of long waiting, the first words which He pronounced were: "The Spirit

of God is upon Me" (Lk. 4:16). Then "the time had fully come" (Gal. 4:4). In Jesus appears the hope of the poor who have searched for the thousands of years of the Old Testament to name this unnamable power which animates everything: "wind, breath of life." Here it is, finding no obstacle or rejection in Jesus, finally showing its true face in the coming of Christ. Through His gaze, His gestures, His words, the whole life and activity of Jesus, it deploys a hurricane which will put the past in full light and will open a radically different era. Th is power, this breath henceforth has a name: the Spirit of the Lord Jesus! Until then, no one possessed the Spirit as He does, "beyond all measure" (Jn. 3:34), but now every person is invited to live in that same transparence (Jn. 3:5). From the very first moment that the Spirit inhabits Jesus, from the breast of His mother whom "the power of the Most High will overshadow" (Lk. 1:35) to His resurrection, His whole life moves under the guidance of the Spirit. During His baptism at the Jordan River, the Spirit reveals to the world that it is Jesus, the promised Messiah (Lk. 3:22), the lamb offered in sacrifice for our sins (Jn. 1:29) and the beloved Son of the Father (Mk. 1:11). Then, "full of the Holy Spirit," Jesus is led into the desert (Lk. 4:1). His mission begins: under this powerful impulse, He confronts the demon, frees His victims (Mt. 12:28), travels across the country, performs miracles, conquers evil and death, speaks "with authority," manifests everywhere an extraordinary familiarity with God His Father and unveils His way of being. It is also in the Spirit that He "rejoices" (Lk. 10:21), and that He is "deeply moved and troubled" (Jn. 11:33). Finally, at the moment of His death, He "gives up His spirit" (Jn. 19:30), which is the prelude to the outpouring of the Spirit upon all humanity.

What are the ways of God hidden under these actions and gestures of Jesus, and what do they announce? Freedom! His name — Savior, Liberator — and His message intermingle: "the Spirit of the Lord is upon Me, because He has anointed me to preach good news to the poor. He has sent me to proclaim release to the captives and recovering of sight to the blind, to set at liberty those who are oppressed …" (Lk. 4:18). For "where the Spirit of the Lord is, there is freedom" (2 Cor. 3:17), and Jesus announces only that which possesses Him also.

His horizons are so free that He disorients all established plans, all logic and careful calculations. In this world, where the strongest build up their powers to better oppress and put aside the little ones, His freedom declares: "Blessed are the poor in spirit, the meek, those who hunger and thirst after righteousness" (Mt. 5:1–11). In a religion where the leaders are themselves "hypocrites and liars" (Mt. 23), Jesus places love over everything else, for freedom is the daughter of love. But the fullness of freedom is love of one's enemies: "You have heard that it was said, 'You shall love your neighbor and hate your enemy.' But I say to you, love your enemies and pray for those who persecute you, so that you may be sons of your Father who is in heaven" (Mt. 5:43–45). This stupendous freedom of forgiveness, this wild love of humanity will lead Him to the cross, but He receives even His death in a supreme act of liberty. Truly "God chose what is foolish in the world to shame the wise" (1 Cor. 1:27).

This radical overturning makes the freedom of the Spirit explode throughout the life of Jesus, who thereby inaugurates a new way of being and an entirely new concept of humanity.

Jesus' nonconformity is absolute. He constantly refines the consciousness of His entourage which is transfixed in laws and institutions that kill life. He is a wandering teacher, with no money, "with nowhere to lay His head" (Mt. 8:20), enjoying happy gatherings and the company of sinners (Mt. 9:9–11), completely independent of all constraints, shaking loose the chains of ownership and personal interest.

He passes by, unseizable and free as the wind, through all the complex structures of duty and obligation. Jesus defies slavery on all levels. For Him, if money becomes slavery, it must be rejected (Mt. 6:24), if the hand or the eye deprives a person of his freedom, it must be plucked out (Mt. 5:29–30). Though He stayed with His mother into His adulthood, He seems to question blood ties in favor of a new community gathered around the word (Mt. 12:46–50). He refuses all the unconditional requirements of the exterior which muzzle the Spirit (Mk. 2:27), even the duty of being good, for God accepts us as we are and His love does not depend on our goodness (Mt. 5:45). Moreover, merits themselves disappear in His eyes, for

God does with what belongs to Him as He chooses (Mt. 20:15) and does not require a salary or a code from which to order or condemn.

Such an attitude of freedom is a menace to all religious principles and systems whatever they may be. Jesus has burned the old law and lifted up the one of love. Thus "Christ is the end of the law" (Rom. 10:4) as He is the end of all religion. "Religion is necessary when there is a wall separating God and man. But the Christ, who is both God and man, has torn down that wall which separates them. He has brought a new life, not a new religion."1 If by His incarnation God has become one with humanity, what is there to "re-link"? "Sin is when we think of God in terms of religion, that is, when we place Him in opposition to life."2 This is exactly the challenge raised by the Jesus Prayer, creating true worshipers who "will worship the Father in spirit and truth, for such the Father seeks to worship Him" (Jn. 4:23).

But in the life of Jesus everything finally culminates in the extraordinary overthrowing and radical renewal which His resurrection introduces. What is seen here is a future for humanity, an almost dizzying freedom: freedom not only from the injustices of the world or the contingencies of daily life, but in relation to the power of death present at the heart of life. For those who know how, in the heart of the prayer, to become conscious of this dazzling reality, the anguish of the future has vanished; God in Jesus Christ has crossed over the abyss of death, and He draws us as of now, in each invocation, out of our hell toward a process of complete re-creation of the universe and of ourselves. The Easter of Christ is the eternal youth of the world, it is our youth rediscovered, not as memory but as future. The decaying world is abolished, eternity is at the heart of time, suffering and death are absorbed by life and the ultimate meaning of all things is revealed in the light and splendor which spring forth from the face of the resurrected One. According to the Fathers, the resurrected Christ is like a "hot coal" filled with the uncreated fire of divinity and whoever comes in contact with Him through the prayer will also be set on fire, torn away from the limits of the earthly self, purified and transfigured little by little, burning with the love of the resurrected Lord and consumed by His joy. Everything is then in our hands: if we accept this gift, we become with Him the only Son, " children of light" (Jn. 12:36).

4. "Son of God"

The Jesus Prayer makes us enter into its Trinitarian density. To proclaim Jesus as "Lord" and "Christ" cannot be truly done without that amazing rapture of the Spirit which we have barely sketched. But to add that He is the "Son of God" is to enter into the mystery of the divine nature: Jesus Christ, the unique Son of God, born of the Father before time; Light of light, true God of true God, begotten, not made, consubstantial with the Father … To pronounce the name of Jesus is to feel something of this unique relationship between the Father and the Son and to place ourselves in the very heart of the Father of whom we know nothing other than the unique word which He pronounces from all eternity: "Jesus" (Jn. 1:1). There, in the heart of the Father, we receive Jesus at His source where He mysteriously originates Himself from the beginning and we receive ourselves with Him: the Father engenders the Son endlessly by nature and He engenders us with Him by grace. It is the same filiation, and that is why we are created "in the image of God." Jesus is our "mold" and, therefore, "the firstborn among many brethren" (Rom. 8:29). The prayer, in making us penetrate deeper into the filial consciousness of Christ, places us before the ultimate meaning of our existence: "What eye has not seen, nor ear heard, nor the heart of man conceived, what God has prepared for those who love Him" (1 Cor. 2:9; Is. 64:3). Yet we carry this fullness on our lips, it is our only way. This "way" is Jesus Himself, for "no one comes to the Father but by Me" (Jn. 14:6). We can understand, then, the invective of Jesus against those who took other filiations, other paths as their source of life: "If any one comes to Me and does not hate his own father and mother and wife … You are of your father the devil" (Lk. 14:26 and Jn. 8:44).

One only needs to go through the Gospel to notice to what extent the presence of the Father was constantly in the heart and thought of Jesus, just as His name was always mixed with His words, and His whole being reflected Him: "Who has seen Me has seen the Father … I am in the Father and the Father is in Me" (Jn. 14:6).

Jesus always invoked the name of God, His Father: "Abba" — daddy, in Aramaic — was His constant prayer, unveiling something of this inconceivable intimacy (Mk. 14:36).

But the Spirit, said St. Paul, also whispers constantly the same invocation in the heart of every baptized person: "Abba! Father!" joining with our spirit to testify that we are children of God (Rom. 8:15; Gal. 4:6). Therefore, through the " Spirit of His Son," the Father makes of us "all one in Christ" (Gal. 3:26–28). By putting the prayer which Jesus incessantly said to His Father in our heart, the Spirit makes us conformed to Jesus in the depths of His interior life, to the point where we can say of the Father of Jesus: "Our Father" with the consciousness of being loved with the same love with which God surrounds His only Son and which makes us similar to Him (1 Jn. 3:1–2). The Jesus Prayer realizes here its true purpose, revealing to us that the depths of our being spring forth in every moment from the Father through the Son in the Holy Spirit. The Life of our life is the divine Trinity. In it we are vitally grafted as a shoot to a trunk (Rom. 6:5).

If we are the children of a same Father, we are, therefore, also a humanity of brothers and sisters: "Everyone who believes that Jesus is the Christ is a child of God" (1 Jn. 5:1). That is why the first fruits of our deification are growth in love and joy. Here we can verify the authenticity f our prayer, the proof that our deification is progressing. Saint John is categorical on this point: "Love is of God, and he who loves is born of God and knows God. He who does not love does not know God" (1 Jn. 4:7–8). Love is the origin and outcome of life, to be born of God and to know Him. "He who abides in love abides in God" (1 Jn. 4:16).

To love is to experience God. The great revelation of Christianity is that this indescribable experience is offered to each one of us and it begins in the very moment in which we decide to believe it and to love, even before anything psychological is felt. "Whoever confesses that Jesus is the Son of God, God abides in him, and he in God" (1 Jn. 4:15). This is instantaneous and objective, and it is in this divine love that we find the face of the divine Trinity.

For God is not three juxtaposed persons: each of the three divine Persons are themselves only in being for and through the other two. Perfectly one and perfectly distinct, community and Persons. Th us the Father is only the Father in giving Himself completely to the Son, and the Son is only the Son in being completely for the Father. It is this act of begetting the Son which constitutes the Father as Person. Each Person is in full reciprocity with the Other. And according to the Fathers, in particular St. Dionysius and St. Basil, the Holy Spirit participates in the generation of the Son, as the Son participates in the procession of the Spirit. Everything is always one and three at the same time in the heart of the divine life.

If the Jesus Prayer did not lead us into a vital familiarity with the mystery which words cannot express, it would lose its reason for being. Nowhere else can we learn to live and to love. To love is to be and to live for the other and through the other, not through and for oneself. Every person, as with God, is found in giving and receiving, for the depths of every being is love, communion. Outside of this there is only darkness and absurdity. The person within us, that which makes us truly human, only awakens through loving, in the act of begetting others, and of being born with them.

To love as the three divine Persons, one must be oneself and want others to be fully themselves. To say "You!" to the other we must find our joy in him through his promotion and our abnegation. And that which is true for the individual is also true for countries, races, civilizations, churches. There is no other social, political or communal program than the life of the divine Trinity, and there is no greater form of existence to which we can attain. For this is resemblance of God! "That they may all be one; even as Thou, Father, art in Me, and I in Thee, that they also may be in Us, so that the world may believe that Thou hast sent Me. The glory which Thou hast given Me I have given to them, that they may be one even as We are one" (Jn. 17:21–22).

5. "Have Mercy on Me, a Sinner"

It is this Life which we call upon so explicitly for ourselves: "me, the sinner," for in the Greek version there is clearly the article. We cannot say of anyone that they are a sinner other than ourselves. We each face God as a unique person, in rupture with our divine filiation. Receiving ourselves from other sources, nourishing ourselves elsewhere than in God, we make of our deepest interior center a place of division where all the divisions in the world find their origin. The external universal schizophrenia is the result of our separation from God within. Everything is divided within us: our intelligence is an atomization of disconnected thoughts and images, in profound disharmony with our heart which, in turn, is attacked by the passions, and in the midst of this despondency our will vacillates between the call of God and the traps of the devil.

"Me, a sinner" is, therefore, the opposite of a selfish turning in on oneself: here our conscience clearly sees that personal and collective responsibility are inseparable. We cannot drown ourselves in the crowd of sinners and justify ourselves by pointing to the wrongs of everyone else! "My sin is ever before me. Against thee alone, thee only, have I sinned" (Ps. 51:4). Each one of our sins is unique and cuts us off from God. This inner recognition is not false guilt which is only disappointed pride, but openness of the heart to God and, therefore, to others. "Me, a sinner" is an impulse of humility which calls upon the tenderness of God. We can bring the sin of the world before God because we have first of all brought to Him our personal sin.

6. "Have mercy"

This cry of despair, if it truly expresses the recognition of our sin, literally opens the "entrails" of God. The entire Bible testifies to this, from the beginning of creation to the death of Christ on the cross for love of the sinner who repents. This is the story of our salvation. And it is only in this stupendous context that we can understand a little of what "have mercy" means when carried by the prayer into the very movement of redemption. The Greek word *eleison*, which we translate as "pity," comes from the Hebrew *hesed*, which means "mercy": we are to God "a darling child." "Therefore, my heart yearns for him; I will surely have mercy on him, says the Lord" (Jer. 31:20). This infinite mercy is the very face of God which He wished to reveal to us through His holy name on Mount Horeb: "I have seen the affliction of my people … and have heard their cry … I know their sufferings, and I have come down to deliver them" (Ex. 3:7–8). God defines Himself as "The One who is" and the One who delivers. And when Moses asks

for pity and forgiveness for his people, God identifies His name with mercy: "The Lord, the Lord, a God merciful and gracious, slow to anger, and abounding in steadfast love and faithfulness" (Ex. 34:6).

To say "have mercy" is to call God by His real name! It is even to reach Him, we might say, in His most sensitive spot, in His maternal fiber, for the word which is at the origin of all the others and contains them all, such as "tenderness," "generosity," "goodness," "pity," etc. is *rahum*, whose root means "maternal breast" and "entrails," a word which constantly comes up again in both the Old and the New Testaments. In His merciful tenderness, God manifests Himself as Father, Spouse, and Mother who cry out: "My heart recoils within me, my compassion grows warm and tender" (Hos. 11:8). He does not resist our prayer for He says: "With great compassion I will gather you" (Is. 54:7). This great and inconceivable love of God for the people who pray that He have pity on them, will only be seen with the coming of Jesus. He is the face of mercy in person who has come from "the tender mercy of our God" (Lk. 1:78) in response to our prayer. The primitive meaning of *rahum*, according to Andre Neher, is of untranslatable wealth and much deeper than the word "mercy": "it leads to the secret of unity which is also the secret of love … Under the eternal nuptial canopy of the love-matrix which *rahamim* evokes, beings are united in an inseparable copresence."3 The word already suggests its fulfillment when it will become flesh in Jesus Christ, in whom God and humanity unite in a same love. Jesus Christ is the beginning and completion of all things, the "New Man" who "makes all things new" (Eph. 2:15; Rev. 21:5). "Therefore, if anyone is in Christ, he is a new creation; the old has passed away, behold, the new has come" (2 Cor. 5:17).

That is why "have mercy" is the cry which all the poor, the sinners, the lepers and the blind, the sick of all kinds and the possessed (that is, the one who I am and who needs to be re-created) send toward Jesus from the beginning of the Gospel to its end! "Have mercy" is the true name of Jesus, the One who saves. "I have compassion on the crowd" (Mt. 15:32), He says and indeed, He is always filled with mercy at the sight of wretchedness. The Gospels show us Jesus touched to His depths several times, filled with an even physical emotion, like an immediate reflex of compassion (Mt. 9:36–14; Mk. 1:41–9:22; Lk. 7:13–; Jn. 11:38–, etc.). And this is how He Himself describes the heart of the Father seeing in the distance the return of the prodigal son. Before the request for mercy, the Father is "seized with pity"; while the son was still "far off," especially spiritually, the Father runs to meet him, throws his arms around him, and covers him with kisses. And in a tremendous explosion of joy, the Father calls for a feast, music and dance. This is a nuptial feast because it celebrates alliance, unity rediscovered (*rahamim*). And he dresses him in "the best robe" and "puts a ring on his hand!" (Lk. 15:11–32). There is undoubtedly no more beautiful text in the universal literature of humanity.

In describing the heart of His Father, Jesus describes Himself. And this overwhelming joy of God for His creature who repents will be fulfilled in Jesus' resurrection. The sinner washed in the blood of the cross, participates henceforth in this divine joy: "Enter into the joy of your Master!" (Mt. 25:21). And, though a sinner, he is saved, his life is no longer that of a person condemned to death, but of a resurrected one. It is feast, music and dance. This resemblance to God will give him, then, the same "compassion" which he will "put on" (Cor. 3:12) in turn to incarnate Christ and His work in the world. For "we ought to lay our lives down for the brethren. But if anyone has the world's goods and sees his brother in need, yet closes his heart against him, how does God's love abide in him?" (1 Jn. 3:17).

213

Love calls forth love, unity and resemblance: "Be merciful, even as your Father is merciful" (Lk. 6:36). Outside of this, there is no "perfection" or "happiness." The Jesus Prayer finds here its final verification, where the gestures of the hands link with the seizing of the heart. The inner sacrament which is the prayer becomes the sacrament of the neighbor: "In the name of Jesus Christ, walk!" (Acts 3:6).

At the end of this book, we find that with which we began, the prophecy of Joel: "All who call upon the name of the Lord shall be delivered" (Joel 2:32). All those who recognize in Jesus the perfect realization of this prophecy become His disciples, His brothers and sisters and constitute with Him a single body: it is the gathering of the messianic community announced by the prophets, "the assembly of the first born who are enrolled in heaven" (Heb. 12:23), the Church. At the heart of desperate humanity, the Church is the sacrament of the resurrected One, the leaven in the bread and the place for rebirth where, while respecting the tragic liberty of each person, it prays so that all might be saved:

LORD JESUS CHRIST, SON OF GOD,
HAVE MERCY ON ME, A SINNER.

15470491R00120

Printed in Great Britain
by Amazon